GOVERNMENT REGULATION OF EMPLOYMENT DISCRIMINATION

A Sourcebook for Managers

Richard Trotter, J.D., Ph.D.
Susan Rawson Zacur, D.B.A.
University of Baltimore

UNIVERSITY
PRESS OF
AMERICA

LANHAM • NEW YORK • LONDON

Copyright © 1986 by

University Press of America,® Inc.

4720 Boston Way
Lanham, MD 20706

3 Henrietta Street
London WC2E 8LU England

Library of Congress Cataloging in Publication Data

Trotter, Richard.
  Government regulation of employment discrimination.

  Bibliography: p.
  Includes index.
  1. Discrimination in employment—Law and legislation
—United States.   I. Zacur, Susan Rawson.   II. Title.
KF3464.T76   1986   344.73'01133   85-29581
                          347.3041133
ISBN 0-8191-5194-7 (alk. paper)
ISBN 0-8191-5195-5 (pbk. : alk. paper)

Acknowledgment

The authors would especially like to thank Madeline Stiffler for her dedication and energy in typing the original manuscript and for her patience and precision in accomodating our many revisions.

Table of Contents

Preface

The work that follows is a compilation of research and writing done by the authors over the past three years. Richard Trotter has written a book entitled, Law, Business and Society-The Legal Environment of Business to be published by Houghton-Mifflin Company, which served as the basis for some sections. Trotter and Zacur have written articles on employment discrimination law with guidelines for practice for a number of publications as noted at the beginning of relevant chapters. All work has been revised and updated for this volume, but the authors remain grateful to the publishers who first put forth their work.

Chapter I

Historical Development of Employment Discrimination Law

Employers today must understand and comply with a number of Federal laws and regulations in the area of employment discrimination. This book will highlight the provisions of the major laws and provide guidelines for employment practices in compliance with these laws. The laws to be discussed are summarized in Exhibit 1.1. The historical development of discrimination law that follows will help to put these laws into perspective.

Post Civil War Constitutional Amendments and the Civil Rights Act of 1866

The roots of legislation prohibiting discrimination in employment because of one's race go back to the post Civil War amendments to the Constitution and the Civil Rights Act of 1866.

The Thirteenth Amendment, which prohibits slavery or involuntary servitude, was ratified shortly after the end of the Civil War. With the power granted via this amendment, Congress enacted the Civil Rights Act of 1866 [1] in order to ensure that the political and civil rights of the newly freed slaves would not be abridged. Section of 1981 of this law states that all persons in the United States "shall have the same right to make and enforce contracts...and have...the full and equal benefit of all laws...as is enjoyed by white citizens."

The Fourteenth Amendment, ratified in 1868, was added to the Constitution to further protect the political and civil rights "for all persons born or naturalized in the United States." The most important clauses of the Fourteenth Amendment were the equal protection and due process clauses. These clauses provide that no State shall deprive "any person of life, liberty, or property, without due process of law nor deny to any person within its jurisdiction the equal protection of the laws." Neither the Civil Rights Act of 1866 nor the Fourteenth Amendment had much impact on protecting the civil rights of blacks during the nineteenth and the first half of the twentieth centuries. This was because early cases, dealing mostly with enslavement, limited the scope of protection against discrimination to the political rights afforded to blacks, and not to employment and other non-political forms of discrimination.

1

Exhibit 1.1

MAJOR FEDERAL DISCRIMINATION LAWS

Law	Administering Agency	Employers Covered	Types of Discrimination Prohibited	Powers of Agency	Agency Rules, Regulations and Guidelines
Civil Rights Act of 1866 (42 U.S.C. §1981)	private citizens (no government agency)	all employers	race and possibly national origin	(private litigants may file suit in federal court for damages, back pay, reinstatement and attorney's fees)	
Equal Pay Act 1963	EEOC	employers subject to the federal minimum wage law	sex	investigate, issue determinations, file suit in federal court	has issued regulations
Title VII 1964 EEO Amendments of 1972 Pregnancy Disability Amendment of 1978	EEOC	15 or more employees	race, color, religion, sex, national origin, retaliation or on the basis of pregnancy, childbirth or related medical conditions	issue complaints, investigate, subpoena relevant records, conciliate, issue determinations, issue guidelines and opinions, file suit in federal court (i.e., for injunction, back pay	guidelines on sex, religious, and national origin discrimination, selection procedures, affirmative action guidelines, regulations on procedure and record keeping
Executive Orders 11246 (1965) and 11375 (1967)	OFCCP	employers having contracts or subcontracts of $10,000 or more	race, color, religion, sex, national origin	investigate, make "affected class" determinations and order back pay, conciliate, cancel, terminate or suspend contracts, debar from receiving future contracts	regulations on enforcement and selection procedures affirmative action plans, sex, national origin and religious discrimination, regulations requiring anti-discrimination postings
Age Discrimination in Employment Act (ADEA) 1967	EEOC	20 or more employees in industries affecting commerce	persons aged 40-70 (with exceptions)	investigate, require production of documents and witnesses, conciliate, file suit for damages and injunctive relief	has issued regulations

2

Exhibit 1.1

MAJOR FEDERAL DISCRIMINATION LAWS

Law	Administering Agency	Employers Covered	Types of Discrimination Prohibited	Powers of Agency	Agency Rules, Regulations and Guidelines
Vocational Rehabilitation Act of 1973	OFCCP	employers with federal government contracts or subcontracts of more than $2,500	handicapped persons	investigate, conciliate (i.e., seek reinstatement and back pay), debar employers from future federal contracts, withhold payments, suspend, cancel or terminate contracts.	requirements for affirmative action plans, enforcement procedures
Vietnam Era Veterans' Readjustment Assistance Act of 1974	OFCCP	employers having contracts or subcontracts of $10,000 or more	requires affirmative action to employ and advance Vietnam Era veterans	same as Rehabilitation Act (see above)	requirements for affirmative action plans, enforcement procedures

3

Executive Orders

No legislative attempt was made to expressly prohibit discrimination in employment until the New Deal era. In 1933 Congress passed the Unemployment Relief Act which provided: "that in employing citizens for the purpose of the Act no discrimination shall be made on account of race, color or creed."[2] Despite the apparently unambiguous wording of this statute, the actual implementation of the legislation was very limited. During this same time, in response to the concerns of civil rights groups, President Roosevelt issued Executive Order 9902 establishing a five member Fair Employment Practices Committee (F.E.P.C.) as an independent agency reporting directly to the President. It was the responsibility of the F.E.P.C. to receive complaints on issues pertaining to race, creed, color or national origin. However, limited staff and enforcement powers resulted in minimal effectiveness. The F.E.P.C. went through various administrative changes until its demise in 1946.

The next President who attempted to address the issue of discrimination in employment was Kennedy. In 1961, he issued Executive Order 10925 which required contractors to take affirmative action to ensure that minority applicants are employed, and that employees are treated equally during employment without regard to their race, creed, color or national origin. This order, like earlier executive efforts to prohibit employment discrimination was limited in scope.

Civil Rights Legislation

On the legislative front, Fair Employment Practice (F.E.P.) bills were proposed from the 1940's to the 1960's but all were eventually buried by the unwillingness of Congress to act. One important obstacle to the enactment of any civil rights legislation was the House Rules Committee, a powerful Congressional Committee dominated by conservative southerners. In an effort to dilute the power of this generally conservative committee, Kennedy, through the help of the Speaker of the House, packed the Committee with additional members sympathetic to the Civil Rights cause.

On June 19, 1963, President Kennedy proposed Civil Rights legislation to the 88th Congress that encompassed a whole range of civil rights issues including equal employment opportunity. The proposed legislation went first to the House Judiciary Sub-

4

Committee which proposed even more stringent legislation for the protection of the civil rights of blacks than did the administration's proposal. However, the administration, fearing that the sweeping recommendations of the Judiciary Sub-Committee would bring about the defeat of the Bill, asked for a more moderate proposal.[3]

After protracted debate and discussion, the Bill was passed by the House and proceeded to the Senate where conservative Southerners fought the Bill vehemently by a filibuster. As a consequence of the intense opposition to the Bill, the enforcement powers of the Equal Employment Opportunity Commission, the agency created by the resulting legislation, were limited. The legislation that resulted, however, was the most significant law that had ever been passed in the United States with regard to employment discrimination.

Title VII of The Civil Rights Act of 1964 as Amended by the Equal Employment Opportunity Act of 1972

The Law

Title VII of the Civil Rights Act of 1964 as amended in 1972 provides comprehensive protection against employment discrimination. Section 703(a) of Title VII states in part:

It shall be an unlawful practice for an employer-

(1) to fail or refuse to hire or to discharge any individual, or otherwise to discriminate against any individual with respect to his compensation, terms, conditions or privileges of employment because of such individual's race, color, religion, sex or national origin; or

(2) to limit, segregate, or classify his employees or applicants for employment in any way which would deprive or tend to deprive any individual of employment opportunities or otherwise adversely affect his status as an employee, because of such individual's race, color, sex or national origin.[4]

5

The 1964 Act also provides however, that:

Nothing contained in this title shall be interpreted to require any employer to grant preferential treatment to any individual or to any group because of the race, color, religion, sex or national origin of such individual or group on account of an imbalance which may exist with respect to the total number or percentage of persons of any race, color, religion, sex or national origin employed by an employer.[5]

Coverage

The 1964 law covered private sector employers, labor unions and joint labor-management committees with twenty-five or more employees, who were engaged in interstate commerce. Under the 1972 Amendments, the definition of employer was expanded to include state and local governments and their political sub-divisions. The minimum number of employees was lowered to fifteen, thus bringing a great many more employers under the jurisdiction of the Civil Rights Act.

Two additional types of employees have been added to groups protected under the law. With the 1972 amendments, employees of educational institutions whose work involved educational activities (teachers and non-professional staff members) were included. In the 1984 case of Hishon v. King and Spalding[6] the Supreme Court held that law firms organized as partnerships are considered employers under Title VII. Thus, employees of other businesses organized as partnerships may also eventually be covered by the Act.

Discrimination

The scope of Title VII prohibits discrimination in employee selection, compensation and fringe benefits, availability of training, development and apprenticeship opportunities, promotion, demotion, dismissal, referral systems for employment, work rules and other conditions of employment.

In order for a plaintiff to prove that an employer's action constitutes discrimination, he/she must show that the specific action taken by the employer was caused by discrimination rather than the employer's business decision-making. The following definitions, when taken together, describe the term as the courts have interpreted illegal discrimination: "discrimination is using race, color, religion, sex or

6

national origin as a basis for 'treating' people unequally ... discrimination is any unnecessary practice that has unequal consequences for people of different race, color, religion, sex or national origin."[7] "Merely because a person in a protected class is affected by a business's action does not make that action discriminatory. In order to prove alleged unlawful discrimination, the plaintiff must show both that he or she is a member of a class protected by an antidiscrimination law and that the employer's action was unlawfully discriminatory."[8] In addition to the above, an employer cannot segregate or classify employees in such a way that women and blacks are channeled into lower paid categories of jobs, while white males with the same qualifications are given access to better jobs. Though Title VII prohibits employers from engaging in a whole range of discriminatory practices, the Act does not require an employer to hire a person just because he/she is a member of a minority group.

Discrimination in favor of blacks against whites would be an example of reverse discrimination. Such action is normally treated as illegal discrimination under Title VII. For example, in the McDonald v. Santa Fe Trail Transportation Company,[9] the Supreme Court held that whites as well as blacks were protected against discrimination under Federal legislation. Reverse discrimination has been a basis for claims of discrimination in some affirmative action cases. This is discussed in further detail in Chapter VI.

The Equal Employment Opportunity Commission

Congress, when it enacted Title VII, created the Equal Employment Opportunity Commission (E.E.O.C.) to enforce the terms of the 1964 Act. The powers of the Commission include the authority to investigate and conciliate grievances alleging racial, religious, national origin or sex discrimination. The complaint had to originate with the person who claimed discrimination, as the law originally stated.

At the time that Title VII was enacted, a number of states had already enacted their own Fair Employment Practices Laws. Thus, in order to accommodate both state and federal policy, Title VII requires all persons claiming discrimination by an employer to file first with the appropriate state agency, if that agency's regulations meet federal standards. After the complainant files with the state agency, he or she must wait sixty days or until the termination of the state proceeding. whichever occurs first. before filing with the E.E.O.C. The statute of limitations on employment discrimination cases is 180 days after the discriminatory act, where no state F.E.P. law exists, or 300 days where state procedures must be followed prior to filing charges with the E.E.O.C. The Commission, after receiving the charge, conducts an investigation and after making findings of fact from the inquiry then attempts to settle the complaint through compromise and concilliation.

Under the 1964 Act, if the Commission was unable to satisfactorily resolve the dispute through conciliation and persuasion, it notified the grievant of his or her right to sue in federal court the party accused of engaging in discriminatory practices. The Court had the right, at its discretion, to waive costs and to grant attorney's fees. The government was empowered to act on behalf of the complainant only if the party engaged in a "pattern or practice" of discrimination. In these cases, the Attorney General of the United States could initiate suit.

In 1972, Title VII was amended. The amended version of Title VII, known as the Equal Employment Opportunity Act enlarged the power of the E.E.O.C. in several ways. The E.E.O.C. itself could litigate court actions on behalf of an individual grievant where conciliation failed. The E.E.O.C. was also empowered under the 1972 Amendments to bring "class action" suits and after 1974 would assume the responsibility for initiation and litigation of "pattern or practice" actions which, under the 1964 Act, had been under the jurisdiction of the Attorney General.

In addition to providing the E.E.O.C. with additional enforcement powers, the 1972 Amendments also provided the resources for instituting suit through the newly created Office of the General Counsel. The General Counsel is appointed by the President with the advice and consent of the Senate. His/her responsibilities include the overall conduct of suits initiated by the E.E.O.C. and the supervision of regional offices.

The national office of the Equal Employment Opportunity Commission is located at 2401 E Street NW, Washington, DC 20507. It is an independent agency headed by five commissioners who are appointed by the President with the advice and consent of the Senate. The commissioners review cases dealing with previously unresolved applications of Title VII as amended and issue guidelines on interpretation of the law. Investigation of charges is generally conducted in regional offices located throughout the United States and litigation in non-compliance cases is handled through the Office of the General Counsel in Washington, DC.

The E.E.O.C. is also responsible for administration of the following:
Equal Pay Act of 1963
Age Discrimination in Employment Act of 1967
Rehabilitation Act of 1973
Executive Orders Relating to EEO
It operates with a national staff of approximately 4,000 and a budget of $150 million. The backlog of unresolved discrimination cases has resulted in a wait of years for a case to be finally resolved by the national office.[10]

If the E.E.O.C. initiates suit, the charges are filed in federal court. The federal court's remedial power can include enjoining the "employer" from continuing to engage in the unlawful practice or issuing orders which may require the employer to hire or reinstate employees who have been discriminated against. The courts may require affirmative action, award of reasonable attorney fees, and may even grant fictional seniority to members of a protected class to make up for past discrimination against the affected individuals.[11] The courts have the power to award back pay, but are limited under the 1972 amendments to back pay damages for a period of only two years. When such awards are made, the back pay amount is generally determined to be the difference between what the complainant would have made, if there had been no discrimination, and what he/she actually earned during the time after the occurance of the discriminatory act.

Processing of a Title VII Charge

A person who feels that discrimination against him/her has taken place must first file a complaint with the appropriate state or local agency. Sixty days later or at the termination of the state or local proceeding, whichever occurs first, he/she may file a complaint with the nearest office of the E.E.O.C. The E.E.O.C. then notifies the employer and proceeds to investigate the charges. The investigation may include written interogotories to the employer, visits to the place of business, interviews with employees and review of employer records. Subpoenas may be issued, if

9

necessary, to obtain relevant documents and information.

If the E.E.O.C. finds a basis for the complaint, then conciliation will be attempted with the employer in order to try for voluntary compliance. If a conciliation agreement is reached it will be binding on all parties after they have signed it and approval has been granted by the E.E.O.C. regional director. Only after conciliation attempts have failed will the E.E.O.C. refer the case to the office of the General Counsel for disposition and/or advise the complainant of his or her right to file a civil law suit within 90 days against the employer. The suit may be on behalf of the individual or as a class action on behalf of all similarly affected parties.

Exhibit 1.2

Steps in Filing A Discrimination Charge

1. Individual or group experiencing an alleged discriminatory act reports its concerns to the appropriate state or local agency.

2. The local agency investigates the claim, advises the complainant on the validity of the claim and, if deemed appropriate, attempts conciliation with the employer.

3. Sixty days after contacting the state or local agency or at termination of that agency's procedures, whichever occurs first, claimant files a complaint with the regional office of the E.E.O.C.

4. The E.E.O.C. notifys the employer and proceeds to investigate the charges.

5. If a basis for the complaint is found, the E.E.O.C. will attempt conciliation with the employer advising on guidelines, case law precedents in similar situations, etc.

6. If a conciliation agreement is reached, it is signed by both the complainant and the employer, reviewed by the E.E.O.C. Regional Director and, once approved, made binding on both parties.

7. If conciliation fails, the E.E.O.C. may refer the case to its Office of the General Counsel for litigation or advise the complainant of his/her right to file a civil suit within 90 days.

Chapter I Footnotes

[1]   42 U.S.C. 1981

[2]   48 Stat. 22.

[3]   Hearings on HR 7152, HR 3139 Before Sub-Committee No. 5 of the House Committee on the Judiciary. 88th Congress, 1st Sess. (1963).

[4]   Sub-Committee on Labor of the Committee on Labor and Public Welfare, U.S. Senate, Compilation of Selected Labor Laws Pertaining to Labor Relations, Part II (Washington, D.C. - Government Printing Office, 1974), p. 610.

[5]   Ibid.. p. 612.

[6]   52 L.W. 4627.

[7]   James Ledvinka, Federal Regulation of Personnel and Human Resource Management, Kent Publishing Company, Boston, Massachusetts (1982), p. 37.

[8]   Henry R. Cheeseman, The Legal and Regulatory Environment of Business, MacMillan Publishing Company, N.Y., N.Y. (1985), p. 741.

[9]   427 U.S. 273 (1976).

[10] Ledvinka, op. cit., p.48.

[11] Cheeseman, op. cit.. p. 747.

Chapter I

Review Questions

Historical Development of Employment Discrimination Law

1. What laws enacted shortly after the Civil War have been applied to employment discrimination cases in recent years?

2. Does Title VII require employers to give preferential treatment to minorities?

3. How does the Hishon v. King and Spalding case discussed in this chapter expand the scope of coverage of Title VII?

4. Can an employer ever refuse to employ an individual because of one's sex, race, color, or national origin?

5. How did the amendments to Title VII enacted by Congress in 1972 alter the provisions of the law?

6. Explain the major steps used to process a claim of employment discrimination.

7. Mr. Jones owns a grocery store which employs ten people. He refuses to hire Jim who is black. Jim files suit with the EEOC. What results?

8. Mary has applied for the job of bank manager of Metropolitan Bank. A less qualified male is hired. Mary brings suit directly in Federal Court. Has she processed her suit correctly?

9. List and explain briefly five major pieces of legislation enacted by Congress to end employment discrimination.

Chapter II

Equal Employment Opportunity in Practice

Title VII has been interpreted by the E.E.O.C. via guidelines on various types of discrimination. Exhibit 2.1 lists guidelines currently available. The courts have relied on these guidelines in many decisions resulting in an expansion and clarification of the law. The following sections will discuss currently recommended practice for employers in the areas of recruitment, testing, selection, seniority, and affirmative action.

Recruitment

Methods of recruitment should attempt to reach qualified applicants of every race, color, religion, sex or national origin. Exhibit 2 provides help for employers in this regard. When placing ads for job vacancies, for example, exployers should examine the demographic data on readership for each newspaper in the region and select a combination of media that is within budget and also reaches the widest qualified audience. Advertising copy should indicate a preference for sex, race or religion only when a bona fide occupational qualification for doing so exists.

When using recruiters, employers should see that educational institutions representative of the qualified population are visited. It is also advisable to send recruiters who are representative of various minority groups. Employment agencies should likewise be representative. Word-of-mouth recruiting (asking employees to refer friends and relatives as recruits) and walk-in recruiting (hiring those who inquire about job opportunities with the firm without specific recruitment efforts by the employer) may be used by employers so long as these methods do not perpetuate an employee population of a single sex or race. If this is likely to occur, then the employer is advised to supplement these methods of recruitment with other methods that can reach a wider audience.

Exhibit 2.1

Guidelines for Employers Available from the E.E.O.C.

On Selection:

Employee Selection Guidelines
Questions and Answers on Employee Selection Guidelines
Record Keeping and Reports

On Discrimination:

Age Discrimination
National Origin Discrimination
Religious Discrimination
Sex Discrimination
Questions and Answers on Pregnancy Disability

Exhibit 2.2

Suggestions For an Open Recruitment System

(1)   Use of minority group members as recruiters.

(2)   Use of employment agencies specializing in referral of minority groups.

(3)   Job advertising in publications aimed at minority groups.

(4)   Participation in job fairs and similar efforts sponsored by minority groups.

(5)   Requesting referrals from the Urban League, N.A.A.C.P., from ghetto job centers, N.O.W., Welfare Rights Organizations, Women's Equity Action League and Professional Women's Careers.

(6)   Actively recruiting in high schools and colleges with substantial minority group or female enrollment. and incorporating special efforts to reach minorities and women in recruiting at all educational institutions.

(7)   Encouraging minority group employees to refer friends and relatives for job openings.

(8)   Formal briefing sessions on company premises and plant tours for minority group organizations.

(9)   Special employment programs for minorities or women. including summer jobs for under privileged students and the like.

(10)   Recruiting brochures that present work situations which include minority groups and females.[1]

To prevent employers from screening out potential employees on the basis of some non job-related trait during the employment application and/or interviewing process, the E.E.O.C. has set forth specific pre-employment inquiries which are per-se in violation of the Act. In 1976 the E.E.O.C. promulgated a set of pre-employment guidelines which employers must follow to comply with the Act. One study has pointed out that:

> These guidelines were prompted in part, by the number of charges filed with the E.E.O.C. and by cases brought before the Courts which have alleged that employers ask questions on applications and in interviews for employment which result in screening out disproportionately more members of a minority group or one sex.[2]

Although a job applicant may volunteer information without liability to the employer, the employer must not solicit proscribed information. Exhibit 2.3 provides some appropriate selection questions for employers.[3]

Among the inquiries which the EEOC feels are illegal are questions about one's marital status, number of children or arrangements for child care. These questions appear to be designed by the employer to discover if a prospective female employee has family responsibilities which, in the employer's view, would interfere with her obligations to the employer. These questions are geared to prospective female employees even if men are asked the same questions. The employers often assume, given past customs within our society, that the burden of child rearing rests almost exclusively on the female.

Another class of questions which are prohibited under the guidelines are those questions which would tend to perpetuate the status quo for the favored white majority. Questions indicating an employer preference for friends or relatives of existing employees are deemed to be discriminatory pre-employment inquiries. When those employed are predominantly white males, such inquiries would continue to deny access to employment for others, thus perpetuating the status-quo.

18

Exhibit 2.3

Appropriate Selection Questions

Area of Inquiry	Appropriate Questions
1. Physical Ability	1. Do you have any physical, mental or medical condition which might, in any way, affect your ability to perform the job for which you have applied?
2. Health	2. Have you had any recent or past illness or operations which might, in any way, affect your ability to perform the job for which you have applied?
3. Citizenship	3. Are you legally employable in the United States?
4. Age	4. Are you over 18 and less than 70?
5. Driver's License	5. For applicants who desire a job driving a company vehicle: Do you possess a legal and current driver's license?
6. Convictions	6. Have you, since the age of 18, ever been convicted of a misdemeanor or felony?
7. Education	7. Did you complete grammar school? High School? College? What coursework did you take that is relevant to the job you are seeking?
8. Extra-curricular	8. While in school, did you participate in any activities or belong to any clubs, which provided

19

preparation for the job for which you are applying?

9. Hobbies and Interests

9. Do you have any hobbies or interests which are directly related to the job you are seeking?

10. Language

10. If a foreign language proficiency is required for a job: What foreign language(s) do you read fluently? write fluently? speak fluently?

Testing

Title VII permits employers to administer professionally validated tests as a condition or requirement for consideration for employment. Title VII states:

> It shall <u>not</u> be unlawful for an employer to give and to act upon the results of any professionally developed ability tests provided that such test, its administration or action on the results is not designed or used to discriminate because of race, color, religion, sex or national origin.

In 1970 the E.E.O.C. promulgated a set of guidelines that employers must follow before a test can be administered. An employment test which adversely affects those protected by the Act cannot be used as the basis for making an employment decision unless "the test has been <u>validated</u> and evidences a high degree of utility. . . <u>and the person</u> giving or acting upon the results of the particular test can demonstrate that alternative suitable hiring, transfer or promotion procedures are unavailable."[4]

The Supreme Court was called upon to interpret the application of the terms of Title VII and the E.E.O.C. guidelines in <u>Griggs</u> <u>vs.</u> <u>Duke</u> <u>Power</u> <u>Co.</u>[5] In the <u>Griggs</u> case, the employer required employees to pass standardized general intelligence tests and possess a high school diploma as a condition of eligibility for promotion. The result of this action was to deny black employees the opportunity to advance to a department where whites, who had not met these standards, were successfully performing the required duties. The employer claimed that the tests were justified on the basis of business necessity, but could not demonstrate their validity (or job relatedness) through established professional validation methods. The Court disagreed with the employer's contention and held:

> The Civil Rights Act proscribes not only overt discrimination, but also practices that are fair in form, but discriminatory in operation. The touchstone is business necessity. If an employment practice which operates to exclude Negroes cannot be shown to be related to job performance, the practice is prohibited.[6]

Thus, the employer's actions were found to be discriminatory. The Court's decision "can be reduced to two principles:

1. Title VII prohibits practices having <u>unequal impact</u> on different race, color, sex, religion, or national origin groups.

2. Business necessity or job relatedness is a defense for using such practices."[7]

Validation

In subsequent cases, the Supreme Court has been called upon to determine the parameters of permissable testing by employers. In <u>Moody v. Albermarle Paper Co.</u>[8] the Supreme Court invalidated the testing procedures used by the company because of the inadequacy of the validation procedures used. Specifically, the company had failed to meet E.E.O.C. guidelines for validation in several ways. The company used supervisory ratings, which is permissible under E.E.O.C. guidelines, but the ratings as administered by <u>Albermarle</u> were too subjective. Secondly, the company used tests for entry level jobs that were validated only for upper level jobs. Additionally the Court held that employers are not only required to validate their tests in the traditional sense, but also must do a differential validity study to determine if the test results are valid for minority persons.

Thus, the Supreme Court has held that a test must not only be job related, but it must also be properly validated. There are three methods by which a test can be validated. These methods were subscribed to by the Supreme Court in the <u>Albermarle</u> decision. They are:

(a) <u>Criterion related validity</u> is a method whereby a criterion such as job performance is measured against a predictor such as an aptitude or achievement test to determine if there is a significant statistical relationship between the predictor and the criterion - i.e., does the person who performs well on the test perform well on the job.

(b) <u>Content validity</u> is indicated where a test respresentatively samples a function to be performed on the job (e.g., a typing test for applicants for a typing position).[9]

(c) <u>Construct validity</u> is a device to determine the degree to which the test measures a certain trait.

For example, a psychological test may be given to police officers where one of the goals of the test is to measure emotional stability, if the test is found to in fact measure the trait of emotional stability, then the test is valid.[10]

The most commonly used method of validation for employment testing is criterion related validity. This is sometimes called job related or empirical validity in the testing literature. The aim is to demonstrate that the test in fact predicts job performance, i.e., a higher score on the test correlates with higher job performance. In some instances it may be possible to justify the use of a particular test because it has been professionally validated for other employee groups with similar characteristics, a technique called validity generalization. However, in the absence of such data, an employer who uses a selection instrument such as a test must be able to demonstrate its job relatedness. Exhibit 2.4 outlines the most important steps in a test validation program.

Exhibit 2.4

Ten Point Validation Program

1. Read Uniform Guidelines on Employee Selection Procedures (1978) Federal Register 43, 38290-315.

2. Perform job analysis or obtain up-to-date job description. From this, establish standards of acceptable performance.

3. Develop measures of job performance.

4. Select predictor measures (tests, etc.) to be used and try them out on current employees (concurrent validation).

5. Perform a pilot study on a sample of job applicants (predictive validation).

6. Repeat step 5 on another sample (cross validation).

7. Establish hiring standards and examine for differential validity.

8. Update statistics yearly for the predictor measure.

9. Examine cut-off scores every 6 months to be sure they are appropriate.

10. Check with the E.E.O.C. and relevant state agency for up-to-date guidelines. Keep records required by the E.E.O.C.

Discussion of The Ten Point Validation Program

The first point is self-explanatory, but nonetheless essential to an effective validation effort. The Uniform Guidelines on Employee Selection Procedures are the foundation for an employer's efforts to validate a selection instrument. The technical standards of acceptability for each type of validation are particularly useful. Another source that can provide guidance is Standards for Educational and Psychological Tests and Manuals issued by the American Psychological Association (APA) in 1973 and the Division of Industrial/Organizational Psychology of the APA's Principles for the Validation and Use of Personnel Selection Procedures (1975). The guidelines are not always controlling as noted by the Supreme Court in United States v. South Carolina (1977):[11] "To the extent that the E.E.O.C. guidelines conflict with well-grounded expert opinion and accepted professional standards, they need not be controlling." Therefore, expert opinion and sources other than the guidelines may be helpful in validation strategy, but it should be noted that the "guidelines will be given preference by enforcement agencies."[12]

Job analysis, the second step, is essential to effective selection procedures. The analysis itself may be performed by a trained job analyst resulting in a formalized, written job description to be used by the test developer. The test developer will usually have to go beyond the job description when defining employee effectiveness in terms of performance standards that can be observed or measured in some way. Working with supervisors and those who know a specific job well, aptitudes, abilities, inclinations, personality traits and behaviors associated with effectiveness should be identified.

Criterion measures are simply measures of job performance for critical areas of employee effectiveness. A common measure is the supervisory rating which can be useful so long as the format minimizes subjectivity and identifies observable or quantifiable behaviors. Other measures may include number of sales or customers served or "widgets" produced or quality control data.

Once the job has been studied and one or more indicators of results have been identified, then predictor measures can be selected. Tests are the most common predictor measure, but others include scored interviews and application blanks, reference checks and biographical inventories. Each potential predictor should be examined for face and content validity. These types of validity are determined by the opinion of "experts" who are familiar with the job and can look over the test to see that it appears reasonable as a selection instrument for the particular job (face validity) and that the questions are appropriate for that job (content validity).

Finally, a third type of validity should be considered at this step, concurrent validity. This involves administering the proposed selection instrument to employees already in the job to determine whether workers who perform well on the job also perform well on the test. If they do not, then the use of the proposed predictor should be reconsidered. If there is a positive correlation for employees at this point, as in Exhibit 2.5, and it is possible to get a sample of 30 or more job applicants, then step 5 may be undertaken.

Empirical, Predictive or Criterion-Related Validity involves testing a sample of job applicants (n=30 or more for statistical purposes). Typically, the test is administered as part of the selection process along with other previously used screening techniques such as interviews, application blanks and/or other tests. The scores on the test being validated are kept secret. In fact, it is recommended that the completed tests be collected, sealed in an envelope, held in a secure place and scored only when the job performance data becomes available six months or one year later. Hiring should take place according to previously used decision criteria. At the end of the designated job experience phase, performance data should be collected and examination of the relationship between test scores and performance measures should take place.

There are three things to look for while reviewing the data. First, the strength of the relationship between test scores and performance. Begin by plotting the coordinates for each individual in the sample on a scatter diagram as depicted in Exhibit 2.5. The desirable configuration of coordinate points is eliptical in appearance with lower test scores generally matching lower job performance and higher test scores matching with higher job performance. One statistic commonly used to examine this relationship is the coefficient of correlation. This statistic ranges from -1 (negative correlation) through 0 (no correlation) to +1 (positive

correlation). Generally an r = + .30 or better is
considered a positive correlation for testing purposes.

The second thing to look for is the statistical
significance of the relationship.   Once r has been
computed, it must be determined whether the finding is
due to chance or a true relationship.   The t-test for
statistical significance should yield a probability of
less than .05 (P< .05) so that there is only a 5/100
probability that the correlation is due to chance.   If
statistical significance is found, meaning that the
correlation reflects a true relationship, then the test
may be valid.

Thirdly, consider usefulness or   the amount of
increase in employee effectiveness that will likely
result from using the test. If we normally assume that
an employee has a 50/50 chance of "working out" in a
job, how much better can we do at predicting the
outcome of a hiring decision with the test?   In
addition to the correlation coefficient,   the
employer's selection ratio or selection rate should be
considered.   This measure is equal to the number of
applicants hired divided by the total number of
applicants:

$$\text{Selection Ratio} = \frac{\text{number of applicants hired}}{\text{total number of applicants}}$$

The lower the selection rate (for example 1/35) the
more useful the test will be in identifying successful
performers.   The higher the selection ratio (for
example 20/25), the less useful the test since most
applicants are hired anyway.   Thus, the business
necessity of using a test would be greater with a low
selection ratio.

After the above procedures have been instituted
with encouraging evidence of test predictability and
usefulness, the entire process should be repeated on
another sample of applicants in order to demonstrate
that the findings are real and can be replicated.   This
practice is called cross validation.   It can be simply
performed if the original group of applicants numbered
60 or more. In that case, randomized assignment of the
job applicants to two test groups upon which
statistical analysis may be independently performed can
yield cross validation.

Exhibit 2.5

SCATTER PLOT OF TEST SCORES AND
JOB PERFORMANCE MEASURES

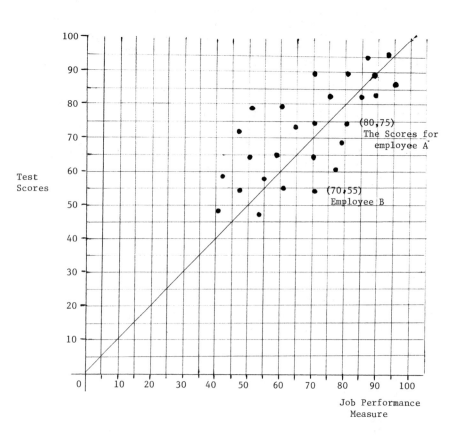

Once a test has passed each of the steps described above, it is considered to be valid for selecting future candidates for the same job. The employer should determine a cut-off or passing score based upon the need for qualified applicants and what is felt to be a reasonable demonstration of knowledge as indicated by test scores. Once a cut-off score has been determined, the selection ratio based on this score should be determined for each sex and minority group represented in the sample. This determination is referred to as differential validity. The employer must be concerned with adverse impact on any protected group as indicated by a selection rate which is less than 80 percent of the rate for the group with the highest rate. This concept will be discussed in a following section on the Four/Fifths Rule. Should a group be adversely affected by the cut-off score, the employer may wish to examine that group's scores to see whether a small change in the passing score might yield a more favorable selection ratio for the group in question.

Once validation is complete and cut-off score(s) determined, the last points deal with program monitoring. Statistics on test scores and job performance should be reviewed yearly because jobs, the labor supply, people, and the employer's needs may change over time. Cut-off scores should be reviewed at least every six months to check for differential validity and trends in scores of the applicant pool (either increasing or decreasing). Further, new guidelines or court cases may occur which impact upon the selection process making monitoring important.

Finally, the employer should check with the E.E.O.C. regarding record keeping and reporting requirements and be sure to comply with them. All records on the validation process should be kept as long as the test is in use and for two years more in cases of an E.E.O.C. inquiry.

Test Administration

Test administration is also an issue for employers concerned with bias-free selection. Administration procedures should be carefully pre-planned so that all applicants or test-takers are treated equally throughout the testing process. Instructions for test takers should be standardized and clearly presented preferably in both oral and written form. If language is a problem for some applicants, consideration should be given to providing tests in

Spanish with Spanish instructions, for example, if appropriate to the employer's business needs. Each test taker should be given the same kind of chair, lighting, and ventilation, pencil, examination book and answer sheet. A time limit may be imposed, but it should be a fair one allowing for sufficient time for completion of the test by at least 90 percent of test takers. Each test taker should leave the test situation feeling that he/she had a fair and equal chance to compete on the test.

The Four-Fifths Rule

If a standardized test is administered by an employer and the test results are such that a larger proportion of minority applicants who take the test fail it than whites, it can be said that the test may have a discriminatory impact on minorities. In 1978, as part of the Uniform Guidelines on Employment Selection Procedures, the E.E.O.C. formulated the so-called Four-Fifths Rule, which was an attempt to define when a test has a discriminatory impact on minorities.

Under the Four-Fifths Rule, a test can be found to have a disproportionate impact on minorities if less than four-fifths (80 percent) of the minority applicants pass the test in relation to the percentage of white applicants who pass the test. For example, if an employer administers an employment test and two hundred whites take the test and one hundred pass the test and are employed then the pass rate for the whites is fifty percent. Suppose one hundred minority applicants take the same test and only twenty-five pass the test. This test would not meet the requirements of the Four-Fifths Rule because the pass rate for the minority applicants would be only twenty-five percent as compared with the white pass rate of fifty percent. The pass rate for the minority applicants was only fifty percent of the pass rate for the white applicants whereas it should have been eighty percent of the pass rate for white applicants. In order for the test to satisfy the Four-Fifths Rule at least forty minority applicants should have passed the test (.80 x .50 = .40). Thus, if forty minority applicants out of a hundred pass the test as compared with one hundred out of two hundred white applicants, the Four-Fifths standard is satisfied since a forty percent pass rate for the minority applicants is four-fifths of a fifty percent pass rate for white applicants.

While the Four-Fifths Rule is used to determine if an employment test has had a discriminatory impact on employment eligibility, it is considered a rule of thumb and not a hard and fast rule. The E.E.O.C. has explained its position on the Four-Fifths Rule in the following terms:

Q. "Why is the Four-Fifths Rule called a rule of thumb?

A. Because it is not intended to be controlling in all circumstances.

If for sake of illustration, we assume that nationwide statistics show that the use of an arrest record would disqualify 10% of all Hispanics but only 4% of all whites other than Hispanic (hereafter non-Hispanic) the selection rate for that selection procedure is 90% for Hispanics and 96% for non-Hispanics. Therefore, the Four-Fifths Rule would not indicate the presence of adverse impact (90% is approximately 94% of 96%). But in this example, the information is based on nationwide statistics, and the sample is large enough to yield statistically significant results and the difference is large enough to be statistically significant. (Hispanics are 2 1/2 times as likely to be disqualified as non-Hispanics) Thus, in this example the enforcement agencies would consider a disqualification based on an arrest record alone as having an adverse impact.[13]

Seniority Systems

In addition to the forms of discrimination discussed previously, employers are also responsible for policies which, though neutral on their face, have an adverse impact because of past discrimination. The seniority system often has a negative impact on minority groups. Seniority, it has been argued, perpetuates past discrimination because minority groups (women and blacks) have been historically denied access to jobs and have been only recently given access to many kinds of employment opportunities. Thus, as a result of past discrimination, they will have the least seniority and will be first to go in the case of lay offs or work force contraction.

The Supreme Court has had to consider this problem in light of the impact that seniority systems have on minority groups. Section 703(k)[14] of Title VII exempts bona fide seniority systems from the requirements of the Act. However, there are unresolved questions. As one writer has asked, "Does the Section 703(k) exemption for bona fide seniority systems insulate them against discrimination charges, even though the system may be discriminatory in effect?"[15]

Several important cases were decided on this issue in the 1976-77 term of the Supreme Court. One case involved black truck drivers who were hired only for city-driving jobs. There was also a discriminatory transfer policy under which blacks were not permitted to transfer to over-the-road driving jobs. In finding that the company had discriminated against black drivers, the Court ordered that the black drivers be given retroactive seniority to the date they first applied for the job. This remedy was applied, since the Court concluded that by providing them with retroactive seniority, they would be put in their "rightful place" since had they been hired initially, they would have had greater "seniority" at the time of hiring.[16]

The Teamsters case [17] which followed was the more important of the two cases, since the Court was called upon to reconcile the terms of Title VII with the fact that seniority tends to perpetuate past discrimination. The Court held that a seniority system that is adopted without a discriminatory motive, is a bona fide seniority system as provided for by 703(k) of Title VII. The Court went on to say that the fact that the seniority system perpetuated pre-Act discrimination, or even post-Act discrimination does not affect its bona-fide status. Those seeking to question seniority must demonstrate that they were subject to post-Act hiring or transfer discrimination.[18]

In the case of Teamsters v. United States discussed above, the Supreme Court held that "bonafide seniority systems" are not discriminatory under Title VII even if minority employees are subject to layoff with greater frequency than white employees by the application of the seniority system. This will be so provided that minority employees have not been themselves the subject of illegal discrimination. A decision consistent with the holding of the Teamsters case was decided by the Supreme Court in 1984.[19] That case arose out of the following facts:

The city of Memphis, Tennessee, which had been guilty of discriminating against blacks in hiring them for positions on the city's fire department, was ordered in 1980 to hire blacks for at least 50% of all new openings in the department until ultimately 40% of the fire department was black. By the end of 1980, 11.5 percent of the fire department was black.

In 1981, the city suffered from a budget crisis which required that some firefighters be laid off. The city adhered to a strict seniority system in deciding who was going to be laid off. As a result of the application of the seniority system, more blacks than whites were laid off. A lower federal court held that the city could not apply a strict seniority system since the layoffs would result in a decline in the percentage of blacks employed by the fire department. As a result of the judge's order, three white firemen who had greater seniority than the black firemen were laid off. The city of Memphis and the union claimed that the judge had rendered an improper decision by ignoring a "bonafide seniority system."

Justice White, speaking for the Supreme Court, overturned the decision of the lower court and held that "bonafide seniority systems" are protected by Title VII in all cases except those seniority systems which are intentionally discriminatory or where the plaintiffs in the case can prove that they themselves had been the victims of employment discrimination. None of the plaintiffs in the Memphis case could prove that they had been the victims of employment discrimination by the fire department.

The case has been interpreted by some as a major setback for "affirmative action" plans which involve employment quotas. Other experts see the case as having application only to the rigid application of "bonafide seniority systems." In their view, affirmative action quotas and goals would be legal as long as the application of these goals and quotas does not result in the displacement or demotion of White workers.[20]

The Bona Fide Occupational Qualification

Section 703(e) of Title VII provides that an employer can refuse to hire an individual on the basis of sex, religion or national origin where such is a "bona fide" occupational qualification reasonably necessary to the normal operations of that particular business. The B.F.O.Q. defense was intended to be a very narrow one. Some of the exceptions to the general rule prohibiting discrimination on the basis of sex, religion, or national origin would include those

33

situations where the sex or national origin of the employee is an inherent part of the job in question. For example, an employer does not have to hire a minority applicant as a pilot if that person lacks an essential "bona fide occupational qualification" such as a certain number of flying hours. Nor does a producer have to hire a female actor, if the part is a male role. In this instance, sex is a legitimate occupational qualification.

The concept of a sex related B.F.O.Q. was considered in Diaz vs. Pan American Airlines.[21] In this case the discrimination was against a male who had applied for the job of flight attendant and had been refused the job because the airline had stereotyped the job as a "woman's job." The airline had argued that it was necessary to hire only female flight attendants because of business necessity. In this case the business necessity defense was predicated on "customer preference." In addressing itself to the airline's argument that "customer preference" fell within the business necessity exception, the Court of Appeals noted that:

> We begin with the proposition that the use of the word "necessary" in Section 703(e) requires that we apply a business necessity test. That is to say that discrimination on the basis of sex is valid only when the essence of the business operation would be undermined by not having members of one sex exclusively.[22]

The Circuit Court of Appeals concluded by saying:

> "The primary function of an airline is to transport passengers from one point to another and . . .not withstanding customer preference the job of flight attendant is tangential to the essence of the business involved.[23]

Employers have automatically excluded women from certain categories of jobs because of the presumption that women as a group are less able to perform arduous physical tasks than men. To justify the exclusion of women, employers have claimed that the weight lifting requirements of certain jobs come within the B.F.O.Q. exception.

In one case an employer refused to hire women for certain classes of jobs which required the lifting of weights over thirty-five pounds. The policy was found unlawful because the employer had failed to develop a system whereby women would be allowed to demonstrate that they could lift weights of more than thirty-five pounds. In Weeks vs. Southern Telephone and Telegraph[24] the Circuit Court of Appeals required that an employer base his refusal to hire women for certain types of jobs on a factual basis and not merely on a commonly held stereotype that presumed women as a class are unable to perform certain categories of jobs. Thus, under the B.F.O.Q. exception, an employer is permitted to make choices which may in effect exclude minorities. if the employment choice is made because of a bona fide occupational requirement.

Proving Discrimination Under Title VII

When an E.E.O.C. case goes to court, a person who alleges employment discrimination must establish to the satisfaction of the court that he/she has in fact been the victim of employment discrimination as defined by law. A plaintiff alleging employment discrimination can base his/her claim of discrimination on one of three major legal theories which are respectively (1) disparate treatment, (2) disparate impact, and (3) pattern or practice of discrimination. Disparate treatment takes place when an employee can prove that he/she was denied employment solely because of his/her race, sex or some other prohibited reason and that the employer intended to discriminate against the plaintiff. A blatant example of disparate treatment would be an employer's job advertisement stating that "no blacks need apply." A second type of employment practice which a plaintiff can claim as illegal is one which has a disproportionate impact on minorities and women. For example, if an employment test results in a disproportionate number of minority applicants being denied jobs because they have not passed the test, those who have been denied employment because of their performance on the test can make a claim of discrimination based on disparate impact. A general pattern or practice of discrimination occurs when an employer discriminates against a whole class of persons (women, blacks, etc.). Each type of employment discrimination is discussed in more detail below.

Procedure for Establishing Discrimination in a Disparate Treatment Case

An individual seeking to prove that he/she was denied a job because of his/her race or sex has the burden of proving that the employer is guilty of discrimination. A prima facie case against the employer can be made in the case of an applicant for

employment if the following is proved: (1) the person
bringing the suit is a member of a class of persons
protected by employment discrimination laws on the
basis of race, color, religion, sex or national origin,
(2) the applicant applied for a job for which the
employer was seeking applicants, (3) the applicant was
qualified to perform the job, (4) the applicant was not
hired for the job, and (5) not withstanding the
applicant's qualifications, the employer continued to
seek to fill the position with a person of
qualifications equal to or less than the applicant's.
McDonnell Douglas Corporation v. Green.[25] In the
case of an employee claiming that his/her discharge was
based on a discriminatory motive, a prima facie case of
discrimination can be made if the plaintiff can prove
the following: (1) the plaintiff is within the
protected class, (2) the plaintiff's performance on the
job was satisfactory, (3) the plaintiff was discharged,
and (4) the employer hired a replacement for the job
who was not within a protected class.

After the plaintiff presents his/her case, the
employer can rebut the plaintiff's case by establishing
that the plaintiff's denial of employment or discharge
was based on a "legitimate nondiscriminatory reason."
Examples of "legitimate nondiscriminatory reasons"
include the following: (1) the person hired had
superior academic credentials, (2) more relevant job
experience, (3) or better on-the-job performance. For
example, in Peters v. Jefferson Chemical Company,[26]
the employer rebutted the discrimination claim of a
female applicant for a position as a laboratory chemist
by proving that she was denied the position not because
of her sex but because she had not done laboratory work
for several years.

If the employer rebuts the plaintiff's claim that
the refusal to hire or discharge was for some
nondiscriminatory motive, the plaintiff can attempt to
refute the employer's rebuttal by claiming that the
reason given by the employer for the refusal to hire or
discharge was a mere pretext and that the real reason
for the employer's decision was the plaintiff's race or
sex. For example, if a black employee is fired because
of lateness while no white employees have been fired
for lateness then such conduct by the employer, it
could be argued, was a mere pretext for discharging the
black employee.   Strong evidence of pretext is the
application of different standards or sanctions to
employees based on race or sex.

Procedure for Establishing Discrimination in a Disparate Impact Case

Disparate impact cases arise when an employer's apparently neutral employment policy has a disproportinate impact on members of a protected class. For example, if a city requires that all candidates for the job of police officer must be at least 5'9", such a requirement is not inherently discriminatory because on its face no one who meets the height requirement is excluded from consideration. However, in reality the requirement effectively excludes large numbers of persons who are members of the protected classes since women, Hispanics and Orientals are frequently under 5'9".

Disparate impact cases frequently will arise with respect to employment testing. The landmark case dealing with the issue of disparate impact is <u>Griggs v. Duke Power Company</u>, cited previously. In the Griggs case the employer required that all current or future employees possess at least a high school diploma or pass a standardized general intelligence test. Griggs, who was black, neither had a high school diploma nor achieved the required score on the intelligence test. The court found that the employer's requirements for employment had a disparate impact on blacks since the requirements were not job related and a disproportionate number of blacks were denied jobs at the company as compared with whites because of the testing requirements.

To establish a case of discrimination based on disparate impact the plaintiffs must prove that the practice has had a disproportionate impact on members of a protected class and that as a result of the practice members of the protected class are under represented in the employer's work force. Once the plaintiff presents his/her case the employer can defend the contested practice on the grounds of business necessity or the job relatedness (validity) of the test required. Even if an employment test has had a disproportionate impact on minorities, it can still be found to be legal if the employer can demonstrate that a certain level of performance on the test is essential to adequate performance of the job. Testing requirements can be more successfully defended by employers in cases where the job requirements are highly specialized or technical in character. A job such as an airline pilot is one where testing requirements can be held legal even though a large number of minority applicants are excluded. If the employer presents a job relatedness or business necessity defense the plaintiff can rebut these arguments by proving that the employer could have ensured that qualified people were employed by the use of a less discriminatory alternative employment practice.

Procedure for Establishing Discrimination in a Pattern or Practice of Discrimination Case

When an employer discriminates against a whole group or class of people protected by Title VII, a pattern or practice case of discrimination exists. Such cases are usually proved through statistical comparisons between the employer's work force and the relevant labor market population. "The legislature has not established objective criteria in Title VII for determining whether an unlawful pattern or practice of discrimination has occurred (e.g., the percentage of minority workers compared to the percentage of minorities in the relevant population), but has left it to the courts to draw conclusions on a case-by-case basis."[27] Once such a case has been shown, each member of the protected class is considered to be covered eliminating the need for individuals to continue to prove that they, too, were discriminated against.

Employer defenses against pattern or practice of discrimination charges include:

1. that the statistical comparison used is invalid because an inappropriate population was chosen (for example, the position requires highly skilled candidates, therefore defeating the use of general population statistics)

2. there are not enough trained minority applicants for the position

3. living and commuting patterns significantly affect the availability of labor (for example, there is no public transportation to bring minority workers to the job site)

4. other business and job-related factors show a nondiscriminatory explanation of the inference of the statistical evidence.[28]

Thus, employers may defend themselves against pattern or practice charges by accumulating statistics to demonstrate the availability of appropriately qualified applicants within the Standard Metropolitan Statistical Areas (S.M.S.A.) from which they draw their workers. Living and commuting patterns as well as the employer's ability to offer competitive wages and fringe benefits in the relevant labor market are also factors to be used in defense of the employer.

[1] Walter B. Connolly, Jr., A Practical Guide to Equal Employment Opportunity Law, Principles and Practices. Law Journal Press, New York, NY (1975), pp. 49-50.

[2] The National Association of Attorneys General. Committee of the Office of Attorney General, "Equal Employment Opportunity: An Overview of Legal Issues." July, 1976, p. 22.

[3] See also: Rowland, Ferris and Sherman, Current Issues in Personnel Management, Allyn and Bacon, 1983, for appropriate selection questions.

[4] Federal Register, Vol. 35, No. 149 (August 1, 1970), pp. 12, 334.

[5] 401 U.S. 424 (1971).

[6] Ibid. at 431 (1971).

[7] James Ledvinka, Federal Regulation of Personnel and Human Resource Management, Kent Publishing Company, Boston, MA (1982), p. 41.

[8] 422 U.S. 407 (1975).

[9] Henry R. Cheeseman, The Legal and Regulatory Environment of Business, Macmillan Publishing Company, New York, NY, (1985), p. 752.

[10] Uniform Guidelines on Employee Selection Procedures, (1978) in Employment Practices Guide (Commerce Clearing House, Chicago, IL).

[11] United States v. South Carolina, 15 FEP Cases at 1196 (1977).

[12] Kendrith M. Rowland and Gerold R. Ferris, Personnel Management, Allyn and Bacon, Inc., Boston, MA (1982), p. 178.

[13] "Questions and Answers on the Uniform Guidelines on Employee Selection Procedures," 44 Federal Register (March 2, 1979, Question 20).

[14] 42 U.S.C.A. 203(k).

[15] Howard J. Anderson, Primer of Equal Employment Opportunity, The Bureau of National Affairs, Inc., Washington, DC (1978), p. 20.

[16] Franks v. Bowman Transportation Co., 12 F.E.P. Cases 549.

[17] Teamsters v. U.S. (TIME) - D.C. Inc., 97 S. Ct. 1843 (1977).

[18] Ibid. at 1861-1863.

[19] Firefighters Local Union No. 1784 v. Stotts, 52L.W. 4676 (1984).

[20] "Much Ado About a Shift to the Right," Time Magazine, June 25, 1984, p. 63.

[21] 442 F.2d 385 (5th Cir. 1971).

[22] Ibid. at 388.

[23] Idem.

[24] 408 F.2d 228 (5th Cir. 1969).

[25] 411 U.S. 792 (1973).

[26] 516 F.2d 447 (5th Cir. 1975).

[27] Cheeseman, op. cit., p. 745.

[28] Ibid.

Chapter II

Review Questions

Title VII as Applied to Various Types of Employment Practices

1. What types of pre-employment inquiries are considered illegal under Title VII?

2. Explain the ten point test validation procedure.

3. Explain how the EEOC applied the Four-Fifths rule.

4. If a seniority system results in minority employees being laid-off is the system necessarily illegal under Title VII?

5. List and explain the five elements of a prima facie case of employment discrimination.

6. How can an employer rebut an employee's claim of employment discrimination?

7. Distinguish between the concepts of disparate treatment disparate impact.

8. List and explain the major procedures that must be followed to establish discrimination in a pattern or practice case?

9. Plaintiff, a female employee, sued her employer because the employer refused to promote her to a position in its International Operations divisions. Her employer claimed she was denied the promotion because foreign customers would be offended by a woman representative of the firm conducting business on their behalf. What defense can the employer raise?

Equal Pay and Comparable Worth*

A type of employment discrimination that has received special treatment under the law and wide attention by employee respresentatives is the issue of pay equality. This chapter reviews the provisions, case law and actions in practice that pertain to compensation equity. It also discusses the currently unresolved issues in this complex ares.

The Equal Pay Act

The Equal Pay Act of 1963, which was an amendment to Section 6 of the Fair Labor Standards Act of 1938, prohibited employers from establishing wage differentials based on sex. Under the Act's terms, it is unlawful for an employer to pay wages "at a rate less than the rate which he pays employees of the opposite sex in such establishments for equal work on jobs, the performance of which require equal skill, effort and responsibility and which are performed under similar working conditions." Exceptions permitted under the Act include those where a pay differential is a result of seniority, merit or performance under a piece rate system.

While the Act speaks of only similar jobs, it has also been held to apply to wage classification systems which designate certain jobs as "male jobs" and other jobs as "female jobs," where the wage rates for the "female jobs" are set lower than the "male jobs" because the jobs are held by women.

In order for jobs to be considered "equal" under the Act, they need not be identical but can be substantially equivalent. For example, in one case the Court held that the jobs held respectively by the male and female employees were not in fact different. The difference that existed the Court said was based on a job classification artificially created by the company to justify the wage differential between the sexes.[1]

---

*Portions of this chapter first appeared as a paper by the authors entitled "Comparable Worth: A New Direction in the Law of Equal Pay for the Sexes - The Legal and Human Resource Management Issues" published in the Mid-Atlantic Regional Proceedings of the American Business Law Association, 1984, Richard L. Coffinberger and Linda B. Samuels, editors.

What is Equal Skill?

This question has been raised particularly with respect to a comparison of relative responsibilities of nurses aids and the male orderlies. Orderlies have been paid more because of weight lifting responsibilities not part of the nurses aid's jobs. Several judges have held that the weight lifting responsibilities of the orderlies does not sufficiently differentiate their jobs from the nurses aids to warrant a differential in pay.[2]

What is Equal Effort?

The standards used by the Court and the Department of Labor in determining what constitutes more effort take into account not only the number of tasks, but if the tasks (1) require extra effort; (2) consume a significant amount of time of all higher paid personnel; and (3) are of an economic value commensurate with the pay differential.[3]

What is Equal Responsibility?

The standards used by the Wage and Hour Division of the Department of Labor which enforces the law are similar to those used by industry in job evaluations.

Among the criteria utilized are the following:

(1) If one group of employees is required to assume supervisory responsibilities in the absence of a regular supervisor. Although minor differences would not justify a pay differential.

(2) If one sales clerk is delegated the responsibility to make a decision whether to accept customers' personal checks, this would be additional responsibility to justify a wage differential.[4]

The above illustrations have the common denominator of increased employee responsibility which can be measured in terms of the scope of independent decision making and the consequences of those decisions.

What are Similar Working Conditions?

A case involving the Corning Glass Company[5] illustrates some interesting questions as to how sex discrimination can impact on wages. The job of inspector had been held by women until the 1920's when a new production technique enabled inspection to be done at night as well as during the day. However, since women were prohibited under state law from working at night, only men could be hired for the job. This presented a problem for the company, since the job in question had traditionally been held by women and thus paid a lower wage rate. To induce men to take the night shift inspection job, the company paid the male workers a premium pay above and beyond the night shift differential. The Court held that:

> The company's continued discrimination in base wages between night and day workers, though phrased in terms of a neutral factor other than sex, nevertheless operated to perpetuate the effects of the company's prior illegal practice of paying women less than men for equal work.[6]

Comparable Worth

Women have suffered from two types of employment discrimination: (1) pay inequality with men even if they performed the same or similar kind of work, and (2) unequal access to jobs held by men in the higher paying blue collar trades, business management, and professions such as law and medicine. Congress attempted to remedy the inequality in pay issue by the enactment of the Equal Pay Act of 1963. The following year, Congress attempted to remedy the "equal access" type of job discrimination for all groups including women, by the enactment of Title VII of the Civil Rights Act of 1964.

Neither the Equal Pay Act of 1963 nor the Civil Rights Act of 1964 addressed the problem of pay inequity between the sexes where jobs traditionally performed by women are compensated at a lower rate of pay than jobs performed by men even though such jobs require similar or even less skill. Proponents for the elimination of pay inequities between the sexes have proposed the concept of comparable worth as means of promoting equality of pay between job classifications. The concept of comparable worth entails a comparison of the wage and salary structure of jobs traditionally performed by women with those performed by men. An example of the application of this concept would be a comparison of the appropriate rate of pay for a secretary, a traditionally female job with that of a stock clerk, a traditionally male job. When workers of one sex are paid less than workers of another sex for performing work that is not identical but is of similar

45

value to the employer proponents of comparable worth charge that sex discrimination exists.[7]

The terms of the Equal Pay Act provide that an employer is required to pay men and women an equal rate of pay if the jobs they respectively perform are similar or the same with respect to the (1) skill level, (2) effort, (3) responsibility, and (4) working conditions.[8] If a woman can demonstrate that she is being paid less than her male counterpart, with the four factors listed above accounted for, she can make a claim for equal pay under the Act. However, the Act also provides several defenses for the employer to justify a pay differential between male and female employees. The four defenses available to the employer are (1) seniority, (2) merit, (3) an output-based pay system (when pay is measured by quantity or quality of employee output) and (4) differentials in pay based on any factor other than sex.[9] An example of the fourth defense would be an employer's claim that a formal job classification system is based on factors other than sex.

The Equal Pay Act offers limited rights to women who have been subject to discrimination because the scope of the Act deals only with pay inequities experienced by women holding equal or similar jobs to men. Nothing in the Act addresses the denial of access to certain types of jobs which have been traditionally held by men. Further, the Act does not address the problem of women being denied upward mobility because of their sex.

The legal protections afforded women against employment discrimination were expanded with Title VII of the Civil Rights Act of 1964. Specifically, the Act prohibits an employer from discriminating against an individual on the basis of race, color, religion, sex, or national origin. Persons in the protected groups can claim they have been victims of discrimination. if they have not been hired, promoted, given equal pay, or been fired for reasons other than their qualifications or competence.

The Bennett Amendment

Since the Equal Pay Act had been enacted prior to Title VII of the Civil Rights Act, the framers of the Civil Rights Act felt it necessary to include a section in Title VII which explained the relationship between the two laws. In order to harmonize the terms of Title VII with the provisions of the Equal Pay Act, Congress included in 703(h) of Title VII, an amendment introduced by Senator Bennett. The Bennett Amendment states: "It shall not be an unlawful employment practice under this subchapter for any employer to differentiate upon the basis of sex in determining the amount of wages or compensation paid or to be paid to employees of such employer if such differentiation is authorized by the provisions of 206(d) of Title 29."[10] The Bennett Amendment was intended to clarify the relationship between the Equal Pay Act and Title VII. The amendment provides that wage differentiations authorized by the Equal Pay Act shall not violate Title VII.

The Gunther Case

The major case examining the scope of the Bennett Amendment and its impact on the concept of comparable worth is Gunther v. County of Washington decided by the Supreme Court in 1981.[11] In that case, the Supreme Court, while not explicitly upholding the validity of the concept of comparable worth as a legal remedy for women claiming employment discrimination under the Equal Pay Act of 1963 and Title VII of the Civil Rights Act of 1964, did open the door for the future use of the concept in employemnt discrimination cases based on sex. The Gunther case could potentially be a landmark case in the law of sex discrimination because in that case the Supreme Court found that the Bennett Amendment to Title VII did not limit the remedies available to a plaintiff to those expressly stated in the Equal Pay Act. In other words, the court's interpretation of the scope of the Bennett Amendment does not preclude a plaintiff from making a claim of sex discrimination on grounds other than inequality of pay for performing "equal or similar work" as men provided for under the Equal Pay Act.

The plaintiffs in the case were female jail matrons who had the responsibility for guarding female prisoners. Male guards, who guarded male prisoners, received 30 percent more pay than the female matrons received. A job evaluation conducted by consultants hired by the county concluded that the matrons should be paid a pay rate 95 percent of the male prison guards. Notwithstanding the results of the job evaluation, the county set the rate of pay for the matrons at 70 percent of the rate of pay of the male prison guards, who received the rate of pay recommended by the outside consultants.

The plaintiffs' legal arguments rested on the following legal premises: (1) the matrons were the victims of intentional sex discrimination by the county because the county arbitrarily set their wages at a rate lower than male prison guards; (2) the matrons were not receiving equal pay for the same or similar work as performed by men and were thus under the protection of the Equal Pay Act.

The Court found in favor of the plaintiffs holding that the matrons had been the victims of intentional sex discrimination by the County of Washington. However, the court's decision was based on narrow grounds. Justice Brennan speaking for the majority pointed out that the "respondent's claim is not based on the controversial concept of comparable worth."[12] While deciding the case on narrow grounds, the majority opinion did open the door for the Court's future consideration of comparable worth cases brought under Title VII rather than under the Equal Pay Act. Justice Brennan stated in his opinion, "We must therefore avoid interpretations of Title VII that deprive victims of discrimination of a remedy without a clear congressional mandate."[13]

Given the ambiguity of the Court's decision in the Gunther case, the concept of comparable worth as a legal doctrine is by no means secure. What may perhaps be a test case to come before the Supreme Court on the comparable worth issue is a case decided in December of 1983 by a Federal District Court in the state of Washington [14] and its subsequent reversal by the Ninth Circuit Court of Appeals. In this case a Federal District Court had upheld the validity of an employment discrimination claim based on a comparable worth argument. Judge Tanner ordered the state of Washington to redress pay inequities between men and women performing different but comparable jobs.

Judge Tanner based his comparable worth decision on the results of a job evaluation of jobs in the state of Washington which was originally conducted in 1974 under pressure from the American Federation of State, County and Municipal Employees (A.F.S.C.M.E.). Norman Willis, a management consultant, was called upon to make a comprehensive evaluation of state employee jobs. Willis examined the state jobs by giving point values to such elements of the job as (1) knowledge and skills, (2) mental demands, (3) and accountability. Willis' study examined the whole array of jobs performed by state workers. As a result of his study many job categories primarily performed by women were found, on a point scale, to be of equal value to jobs performed by men. While the Willis system provided favorable results for women workers, not all job evaluation systems favor women workers if there are structural biases in the system that give greater weight to factors associated with jobs performed by men such as physical strength requirements and supervisory responsibility.

Tanner also rejected the state's argument that the state had determined the respective rates of pay for the various worker groups on the basis of the prevailing market rate. The differential in rates of pay, the state argued, was not a result of an intent to discriminate but a result of external market forces. Tanner appointed a "master" to determine new pay scales for an estimated 15,000 underpaid "women's jobs." The state of Washington appealed the decision which it claimed would cost the state some $770 million in back pay and $130 million annually to the payroll.[15]

On September 4, 1985, the U.S. Court of Appeals for the Ninth Circuit in San Francisco overturned Judge Tanner's 1983 decision upholding the validity of the concept of comparable worth. The Appeals Court rejected Tanner's decision on several grounds. The Ninth Circuit analyzed the legal grounds upon which the District Court based its decision in the following terms:

"In the instant case, the District Court found a violation of Title VII, premised upon both the disparate impact and disparate treatment theories of discrimination may be established by showing that a facially neutral employment practice, not justified by business necessity, has a disproportionately adverse impact upon members of a group protected under Title VII. Under the disparate treatment theory, in contrast, an employer's intent or motive in adopting a challenged policy is an essential element of liability for a violation of Title VII. It is insufficient for a plaintiff alleging discrimination under the disparate treatment theory to show the employer was merely aware of the adverse consequences the policy would have on a protected group."[16]

The Appellate Court rejected the District Court's finding of discrimination under Title VII, under a disparate impact analysis but required instead that a finding of discrimination must be made under a disparate treatment theory which requires individuals claiming discrimination to prove that the discrimination was based on an intent to discriminate. In this case the court found no violation of Title VII under a disparate impact analysis because the wage disparity between the sexes across different types of jobs in the state of Washington was due not to a conscious intent to discriminate against women by the state of Washington, but rather the disparity was caused by market rate determinations and union bargaining power.

Collective Bargaining and Revision of Job Classifications

Notwithstanding the setbacks to the concept of comparable worth resulting from the decision of the Ninth Circuit case, proponents of the concept have been and will surely continue to seek implementation of pay equity through comparable worth by means of the collective bargaining process and through pressure on state legislatures to enact laws requiring that state employee pay rates be determined on a comparable worth basis.[17]

An example of how comparable worth may be effected through the collective bargaining process is illustrated by the following situation. During negotiations in 1981 between the city of San Jose, California and A.F.S.C.M.E. the issue of comparable worth was raised. The results of a job evaluation conducted by an outside consulting firm showed that based on the use of the city's internal point-factor evaluation system, certain jobs performed by women were comparable in know-how, problem-solving and accountability to higher paying jobs performed by men. The jobs receiving equal points were nurse and fire truck mechanic, librarian and planner, secretary and lab technician. The difference in pay between nurses and mechanics turned out to be 49 percent. The city agreed to work toward pay equality over a 3-year time frame. The workers struck and eventually got a settlement to close the wage gap in two years. The internal wage evaluation system was the focus of comparability. Competitive labor market rates for the jobs in question were virtually ignored.[18]

Revision of job classification systems can also bring about some relief in comparable worth situations. Some traditional job classification systems have been biased against females because the system arbitrarily classified jobs performed by women at lower rates of pay than similar jobs performed by men even though the task content of the two jobs is similar. In a recent case decided by the U.S. Court of Appeals in Washington, D.C. substantial back pay awards were made to women who worked for the Government Printing Office and were paid lower rates of pay because their job classifications were supposedly different from those job classifications of higher paid male workers at the G.P.O. even though the content of their jobs was similar to that of the male workers.[19]

Market Forces

In some comparable worth cases the employer's defense has been that the pay differential was not due to an intent to discriminate but rather that the pay scale of the various types of work merely reflected the prevailing market value of the work performed.[20] The so called market value defense has been attacked by plaintiffs seeking relief on the ground that the use of the labor market salary rates perpetuates past discrimination because women are ghettoed into a limited number of female jobs. Thus, if a nurse is paid by a hospital according to the labor market of the nursing profession, the hospital, by using discriminatory market salary rates, is perpetrating past discrimination.

A federal court case addressed the issue of pay inequities between the sexes on the basis of structural inequities in the market place. The Allstate Insurance Company had a practice of basing the monthly minimum salary for new agents on the basis of their prior earning history irrespective of their ability or education. The practice resulted in female agents receiving a rate of compensation lower than male agents because the female agents often held lower paying jobs prior to their employment by Allstate. The Court did not address the comparable worth issue per-se but held that the company's practice did result in a denial of equal pay for equal work.[21] Thus, as one interpreter of the case has observed: the Court held that an affirmative equal pay defense is not established unless the employer can demonstrate that the entire wage differential is based on factors other than sex. Therefore, when an employer considers an employee's prior salary situation as well as education, ability and experience in setting their current minimum salary, this perpetrates the discriminatory effect of female employees' previous salaries. In this case, the employer did not establish that the minimum monthly salaries of female and male sales representatives were based on factors other than sex.[22]

Position of the E.E.O.C. on Comparable Worth

On June 17, 1985, the Chairman of the Equal Employment Opportunity Commission issued a statement to the press announcing the decision of the EEOC to reject the concept of comparable worth. This decision was based on the results of a study conducted by the U.S. Civil Rights Commission at an earlier date recommending that the concept of comparable worth be rejected, as well as on the facts of a test case presented before the E.E.O.C.

The party alleging discrimination in the case claimed that the employer discriminated against women on the basis of sex because the wage rates for the employer's administrative staff, which was 85 percent female, were less than those paid to the maintenance staff, which was 88 percent male, even though the duties performed by the employees in female-dominated jobs required equal or more skill, effort and responsibility than those in male-dominated jobs. The persons bringing the suit did not claim that the disparity of wage rates between the sexes was a result of intentional discrimination on the part of the employer but rather they based their claim for an adjustment of the wage rates between the sexes on the theory of "comparable worth."

The Commission held that Title VII only protects individuals who have been the victims of employment discrimination based on sex. The Commission found no violation of Title VII in the test case for several reasons: (1) there was no allegation--and no evidence--that the employer assigned employees to jobs on the basis of sex; (2) there was no allegation--and no evidence--that any barriers existed to prevent males and females from moving between job categories; and (3) the disparity of the wage rates between the female and male employees in the case were based on non-sex based decisions of employers, by collective bargaining, or by the market place.[23]

Implications for Human Resource Management

Until the Supreme Court issues a definitive decision or Congress passes legislation on the subject, the viability of comparable worth, as a legal concept, will be subject to a case by case interpretation by the lower state courts. In the absence of federal precedent, sixteen states have enacted legislation calling for equal pay for comparable work.[24] States have required studies of state classified jobs and subsequent adjustments to salaries of women and men whose pay was found to be inequitable. These adjustments have ranged from 6.8 percent to 30 percent.[25]

Since comparable worth is now a mandated concept in some states and since it continues to be an issue before the courts, HRM practioners must be aware of the potential impact on their activities. The Allstate case demonstrated that recruitment can be affected when starting salaries are based upon previous employment history in predominantly female jobs. The San Jose situation emphasized the importance of comparable worth as a collective bargaining issue that may be pushed to the point of impasse. The Gunther decision, as well as others, supported the use of a job evaluation system in determining pay rates. The implications from these and other decisions are as yet unclear although some conclusions may be drawn.

If comparable worth is an important concept to be dealt with, then employers must institute or refine their present job evaluation systems. These systems need to be based on observable, measurable characteristics. Reliance on the subjective judgment of job analysts should be minimized wherever possible. The factors themselves should be examined to be sure that they represent a fair range of attributes and are not weighted more heavily than reasonable toward dimensions more likely to be important in traditionally male jobs.

The collective bargaining area will also be affected. The net result of refined job evaluations could ultimately be that the resulting pay decisions will benefit better educated female and male professionals and technicians at the expense of unskilled unionized workers and semi-skilled tradespeople, whose wages have been increased through collective bargaining efforts.[26] Personnel specialists who believe that wage structures negotiated with a union provide immunity from comparable worth litigation will find that it will be the employer who must defend the logic of wage differentials.[27] Thus, variations in pay will have to be based on factual information about job requirements and have nothing to do with the sex of the job holder or his/her union affiliation.

Finally, human resource planning will be affected. The mix of the labor force could change if the pay attached to certian jobs becomes relatively more or less attractive. If market forces are down

played. then the supply of labor for certain jobs may
increase or decrease solely in response to changes in
expected salary. Further, as labor costs increase due
to comparable worth adjustments. the firm's ability to
maintain the current number of workers may be affected
by constrained budgets. Astute planners will take this
into account in re-evaluating all future human resource
assignments.[28]

This chapter has attempted to define the concept
of comparable worth, trace its legal development, and
identify current issues of concern to practioners.
Although comparable worth has not been mandated by
legislation at the federal level, and the courts have
questioned its validity, states and even voluntary
efforts are giving the concept practical meaning. The
evidence suggests that comparable worth will continue
to be a focus of concern and will surely be a
significant employment issue for the 1980's.

[1] Shultz v. Wheaton Glass Company, 421 F.2d 259.

[2] F.E.P. 421:305.

[3] Hodgson v. Brookhaven General Hospital, 9 F.E.P. Cases 579.

[4] F.E.P. 401:483 - Wage-Hour Division.

[5] Corning Glass Works v. Brennan, 417 U.S. 191, 1974.

[6] Ibid. at 209.

[7] Women, Work and Wages: Equal Pay for Jobs of Equal Value (Washington, D.C., National Academy Press, 1981), p. 9.

[8] 29 U.S.C. Sec. 201 et. seq. (1976).

[9] Ibid.

[10] 42 U.S.C. Sec. 2000 (e)-2(h) (1976).

[11] 452 U.S. 161 (1981).

[12] Ibid. p. 178.

[13] Ibid.

[14] American Federation of State, County and Municipal Employees v. State of Washington.578 F. Sup. 846 (1983).

[15] Jane Bryant Quinn, "Comparable Pay for Women," Newsweek, January 16, 1984.

[16] American Federation of State, County, and Municipal Employees, AFL-CIO, CAFSCME v. State of Washington, United States Court of Appeals for the Ninth Circuit, Slip Opinion, September 4, 1985.

[17] Amy Winientz, "Back to the Bargaining Table," Time, September 16, 1985.

[18] James T. Brinks. "The Comparable Worth Issue: A Salary Administration Bombshell," Personnel Administrator, November 1981, pp. 37-40 and Michael F. Carter, "Comparable Worth an Idea Whose Time Has Come?" Personnel Journal, October 1981, p. 792.

[19] Thompson v. Sawyer, 678 F.2d257 (CA-D of C. 1982), 94 L.C. Sec 34, 186.

[20] see Judy B. Fulghum, "The Employer's Liabilities Under Comparable Worth," Personnel Journal, May 1983, p. 404.

[21] Kouba v. Allstate Insurance Company, 523F. Supp. 148 (D.C. Cal. 1981).

[22] Clarence Thomas, "Pay, Equity and Comparable Worth," Labor Law Journal, January 1983, Vol. 34, No. 1, p. 11.

[23] "E.E.O.C. Rejects Comparable Worth," Ideas and Trends in Personnel. Human Resources Management, Illinois Commerce Clearing House, July 12, 1985, p. 112.

[24] Alice H. Cook, "Comparable Worth: Recent Developments In Selected States," Labor Law Journal, August 1983, p. 494-504.

[25] Ibid.

[26] Richard J. Schonberger and Harry W. Hennessey, Jr., "Is Equal Pay for Comparable Worth Fair?" Personnel Journal, December, 1981, p. 968.

[27] David Wainwright, "Why Equal Pay is Dynamite for Pay Structures," Personnel Management, October, 1983, p. 51.

[28] Karen S. Koziara, David A. Pierson and Russell E. Johannesson, "The Comparable Worth Issue: Current Status and New Direction," Labor Law Journal, August 1983, p. 504-9.

Review Questions

Equal Pay and Comparable Worth

1. How did the issue of comparable worth arise from the Equal Pay Act?

2. What is the relationship between the Bennett Amendment and the Equal Pay Act?

3. Explain the concept of comparable worth in terms of the following issues:
    (a) job evaluation
    (b) job classification systems
    (c) market forces

4. Both males and females were employed by two banks as bookkeepers and tellers. The females holding these positions were paid substantially less than males holding the same job. However, the males in addition to performing their bookkeeping and bank teller duties were also involved in an informal unwritten training program where they were rotated from department to department. Were the pay differentials a violation of the Equal Pay Act? Was the training program a "fact other than sex"?

Chapter IV

Equal Employment Opportunity and Employment Benefits*

Employment or fringe benefits are those forms of non-direct compensation that enhance an employer's ability to attract and retain qualified personnel. This chapter will examine the areas of maternity and pension benefits. These areas have experienced scrutiny for sex bias with resulting legislation and court interpretations to serve as guides for employer policy.

The Pregnancy Disability Amendment

On October 31, 1978, the Pregnancy Disability Amendment was enacted into law as Section 701 (K) of Title VII of the Civil Rights Act of 1964.[1] This section examines the socio-legal developments preceding passage of the Pregnancy Disability Amendment, the basic provisions of the act, and finally its impact upon employers, employees, and unions.

In Muller v. Oregon[2] the Supreme Court upheld "protective" labor laws for women workers after having rejected similar protection for men. In rendering its 1908 decision, the Supreme Court reasoned that it was necessary to place women "properly" in a class by themselves for legislative purposes. The Court went on to emphasize that the biological differences between the sexes, made it necessary for the states to give special protection for women from work related injuries. On this point the Court reasoned:

> As healthy mothers are essential to vigorous offspring, the physical wellbeing of women becomes an object of public interest and care in order to preserve the strength and vigor of the race.[3]

After this decision was rendered, a number of states enacted laws regulating the conditions of employment for women.

---

*Portions of this chapter are adapted from two articles by the authors' "The Pregnancy Disability Amendment: What the Law Provides," Personnel Administrator, Part I, February, 1982, p. 47-54 and Part II, March, 1982, p. 55-58.

Labor Force Statistics on Women

The number of women in the workplace has increased dramatically since 1908 when Muller v. Oregon was decided. Less than 20 percent of all women 25-64 years of age were regularly active in the labor force around the year 1900 compared to an overall female labor force participation rate of over 52 percent currently.[4] In fact, as of 1980, there were nearly 10 million female family heads (widowed, separated, divorced and single) and more than 6 of every 10 were regularly active in the labor force. Nearly 70 percent of these female family heads with children under the age of 18 worked consistently. Recent U.S. Labor Department data indicate that 6 million women head families with children under 18 while working outside the home and 1.3 million working mothers have children under 6 years of age for a participation rate of 62 percent.[5]

Regular labor force participation appears to be related to educational attainment and marital status in recent statistics on working women. The labor force participation rate of women with 4 years of high school exceeded 57 percent, while nearly 7 out of 10 women with 4 years or more of college were working in 1979.[6] Among never-married, separated and divorced women, labor force participation was even higher, ranging from 70-80 percent for women with 4 years of high school and 83-86 percent for those with 4 or more years of college.[7] Thus, the question of equality of treatment in access to jobs as well as equality of treatment in the terms and conditions of employment has become an increasingly important area of study. Since women now have greater access to jobs, focus of attention has shifted to not only providing equality of opportunity for jobs but also providing equality in the pay and benefits packages for such jobs.

Fringe Benefits

Fringe benefits were introduced into the employment relationship in the early 1920's for the purpose of keeping workers on a long-term basis. Since employers regarded women as temporary workers who would marry, have children and leave the labor force, benefit packages were tailored to the needs of the longer service male employees. As one commentator observed:

> From its inception, there was evidence
> that in fringe benefits as well as in
> other terms and conditions of employment
> the employer's view of women as marginal

workers whose proper and expected role was wife and mother resulted in limitation of the benefits made available to them.[8]

As of 1964, forty percent of all employers still did not provide for maternity leave, preferring instead to simply terminate pregnant women.[9] Title VII and affirmative action programs under Executive Orders 11246 and 11375 did encourage many employers to change their policies as evidenced by 1973 statistics showing that 73 percent of women workers, requiring such benefits, received maternity leave accompanied by re-employment rights. Twenty-six percent of eligible women were able to use sick leave for pregnancy-related illness and disability.[10]

Title VII and Pregnancy

However, after 1973, several decisions by the Supreme Court threatened to roll back the progress that had been made as a result of the enactment of Title VII with respect to requiring an employer to treat pregnancy as any other employee disability. The issue of the exclusion of pregnancy disability from employee health plans was brought before the Courts under the terms of Title VII of the Civil Rights Act of 1964, Section 703 as described in Chapter I.

The Supreme Court was first called upon to interpret terms of Title VII relevant to pregnancy in Phillips vs. Martin Marietta Corp.[11] In that case the Supreme Court was asked to render a decision on so-called "sex plus" employment policies which deny employment to women on the basis of sex related characteristics and stereotypes. Thus, female employees are treated differently by the employer not only because of their sex per-se but because of some characteristics associated with the role assigned to women. In the Philips case, the petitioner brought suit because the employer had instituted a policy whereby it refused to accept employment applications from women with pre-school age children.

The case presented some unusual issues since the employer presented evidence that it did not discriminate against women in employment, especially for the job that the petitioner had sought. In fact the employer presented evidence that 80 percent of the employees in the position for which the petitioner had applied were women. Thus, the question was no longer just a question of pure sex discrimination, but rather dealt additionally with employment policies which discriminate against women, because of sex roles such as family rearing. The Supreme Court held that:

> The existence of such conflicting family obligations, if demonstrably more relevant to job performance for a woman, than for a man would arguably be the basis for distinction under 703(a) of the Act and therefore an illegal form of sex discrimination.[12]

The courts have decided a number of cases in which women were treated differently not only because of their sex, but because they were burdened with the additional responsibilities of child-rearing which the employer regarded as an impediment to effective performance on the job. In Sprogis vs. United Airlines, Inc.,[13] a circuit court held that an Airline's denial of employment to married females, while not encumbering males with such discrimination constituted an act of sex discrimination as defined by Title VII. Thus, the Circuit Court made clear that Title VII's prohibition against sex disscrimination included discrimination because of sex related responsibilities.

In the case of General Electric vs. Gilbert[14] the Supreme Court ruled that the exclusion of pregnancy from an employer's disability benefit plan did not constitute sex discrimination under Title VII of the Civil Rights Act of 1964. The Court was also called upon to decide if the E.E.O.C. Guidelines on discrimination because of sex were violated by the policies of the General Electric Company with respect to excluding pregnancy from disability coverage. The Court considered that the guidelines were not entitled to great weight.[15] The Court went on to reason "that the exclusion of pregnancy from coverage under a disability benefits plan was not in itself discrimination based on sex."[16] Rather, the Court reasoned

> as there is no proof that the package is in fact worth more to men than to women, it is impossible to find any gender based discriminatory effect in this scheme simply because women, disabled as a result of pregnancy do not receive benefits; that is to say, gender-based discrimination does not result simply because an employer's disability plan is less than all inclusive.[17]

In Nashville Gas Co. vs. Satty[18] the plaintiff
alleged that the denial of sick pay for mandatory
pregnancy leave and deprivation of accrued seniority
after return from leave violated both Section 703 (a)
(1) and 703 (a) (2). As in Gilbert the Court held that
the exclusion of pregnancy from the sick leave plan did
not constitute intentional discrimination and that the
plaintiff had failed to show any disproportionate
adverse impact. The Court again suggested that the
doctrine of disproportionate adverse impact did not
apply to claims under Section 703 (a) (1), adding that
claims of discrimination in sick leave or disability
plans could be brought only under that section. The
Court also found that the deprivation of accrued
seniority after pregnancy leave did not constitute
intentional discrimination. The Court, however, did
hold in Satty that:

> . . . the company's policy of depriving
> employees returning from pregnancy leave
> of their accumulated seniority acts both
> to deprive them of "employment
> opportunities" and to adversely affect
> their status as an employee. The
> company's policy denied (plaintiff)
> specific employment opportunities that she
> otherwise would have obtained. Even if
> she had ultimately been able to regain a
> permanent position with petitioner, she
> would have felt the effects of a lower
> seniority level, with its attendant
> relegation to less desirable and lower
> paying jobs for the remainder of her
> career with the company.[19]

It can be seen from the preceding historical
review of the socio-legal development of pregnancy-
related decisions that Title VII, as enacted in 1964,
was intended to extend employment protection to women
with respect to pregnancy. Since the Supreme Court
rejected the argument that the denial of pregnancy
disability leave by employees constituted sex
discrimination under Title VII, Congress responded to
this situation by amending Title VII in 1978 to require
employers with health plans to include pregnancy as a
covered disability.

The 1978 Amendment

The Pregnancy Disability Amendment to Title VII
of the Civil Rights Act of 1964 (Section 701 (K), 1978)
broadened the definition of sex discrimination to

encompass pregnancy, childbirth, or related medical
conditions.[20] By Amendment to Title VII, Section 701
(K) therefore provides that it shall be an unfair
employment practice for an employer to discriminate on
the basis of pregnancy, childbirth, or related medical
conditions in hiring, promotion, suspension, discharge
or in any other term or condition of employment.
Treating abortion separately, the amendment states that
employers are not required to pay health insurance
benefits for abortion except where the life of the
mother would be in danger if the fetus were carried to
term or where "medical complications" have arisen from
abortion. An employer may provide abortion health
insurance benefits voluntarily or if required to do so
by a union-management contract, however.

Although the law is brief in its language, it is
quite extensive in its interpretation. For example,
with regard to leave procedures, an employer cannot
require women to take leave at an arbitrarily set time
in their pregnancy. When leave is required, it is
determined on the basis of the time when the individual
woman is no longer able to work. The employer is also
required to grant full reinstatement rights to women on
leave for pregnancy related reasons, including credit
for previous service and accrued retirement benefits as
well as accumulated seniority. Additionally, the law
prohibits an employer from failing to pay for
disability or sick leave for pregnancy, childbirth or
related medical conditions in the same manner as it
pays for other employee disability or sick benefits.
However, an employer will not have to allow pregnant
women to use paid sick leave or to receive disability
benefits merely because they are pregnant. Benefits
will have to be paid only on the same terms applicable
to other employees--namely, only when the employee is
medically unable to work.[21] The Amendment prohibits
an employer from failing to pay medical and hospital
costs for childbirth to the same extent that it pays
for medical and hospital costs for other conditions.
If there is a maximum for comparable medical or
surgical or hospital procedures, the maximum should be
no less for medical or hospital costs relating to
pregnancy or childbirth.[22]

The Pregnancy Amendment to Title VII thus
expanded the scope of Title VII protection to encompass
under sex discrimination, employer policies which
discriminate in conferring disability benefits on the
basis of pregnancy, childbirth, or related medical
conditions. Additionally the Amendment applies to all
aspects of the employment relationship including--

hiring, reinstatement, termination, sick leave, medical benefits, seniority and other conditions of employment.

The Act was intended to prevent discrimination on the basis of pregnancy but does not require that pregnant employees be given special treatment. Addressing this question the authors of the House of Representatives Report on the Amendment have noted that:

> It must be emphasized that this legislation, operating as part of Title VII, prohibits only discriminatory treatment. Therefore, it does not require employers to treat pregnant employees in any particular manner with respect to hiring, permitting them to continue working, providing sick leave, furnishing medical and hospital benefits providing disability benefits or any other matter.
>
> The bill in no way requires the institution of any new programs where none currently exist. The bill would simply require that pregnant women be treated the same as other employees on the basis of their ability or inability to work.
>
> The "same treatment" may include employer practices of transferring workers to lighter assignments, requiring employees to be examined by company doctors or other practices so long as the requirements and benefits are administered equally for all workers in terms of their actual ability to perform work.[23]

Impact of the Law

Enforcement of the Pregnancy Disability Amendment, as with other Title VII provisions, is carried out by the Equal Employment Opportunity Commission (E.E.O.C.). The E.E.O.C. issued guidelines on the law in April, 1979, in order to clarify compliance procedures for covered employers (businesses, local and state governments with 15 or more employees). The guidelines outline procedures for compliance with the points of law outlined in the previous sections.

Enforcement of the Pregnancy Disability Amendment, as with other Title VII provisions, is carried out by the Equal Employment Opportunity Commission (E.E.O.C.). The E.E.O.C. issued guidelines on the law in April, 1979, in order to clarify compliance procedures for covered employers (businesses, local and state governments with 15 or more employees). The guidelines outline procedures for compliance with the points of law outlined in the previous sections.

An employer in compliance with the Pregnancy Disability Amendment to Title VII amended its health insurance plan so that pregnancy related conditions of female employees were covered to the same extent as other types of medical conditions. The plan also provided coverage of the pregnancy-related conditions of the spouses of male employees, but the pregnancy coverage received by the wives of male employees was less than that received by female employees.

A male employee filed a charge with the EEOC claiming that the employer's health insurance plan's provision respecting the coverage for Pregnancy Disability constituted an illegal form of sex discrimination under Title VII and the Pregnancy Disability Amendment. The EEOC upheld the employee's claim. The employer appealed the case to a federal district court which reversed the EEOC's holding and held that the employer's plan did not constitute an illegal form of sex discrimination against male employees because the Pregnancy Disability Amendment was enacted for the purpose of protecting female employees from discrimination and did not cover the spouces of male employees.

The Supreme Court reversed the lower Court's holding, in doing so the court reasoned that the employer's differential treatment of the coverage of female employees constituted an illegal form of sex discrimination since the distinction made by the employer was gender based discrimination protected by the terms of the act. The court also held that Title VII extends protection against sex discrimination to the pregnant spouse of male employees, which is also discrimination against male employees.[24]

Discussion of the impact of the Pregnancy Disability Amendment will now proceed to review personnel actions, leave and reinstatement policies, medical and disability benefit payments and union relations. Examination of these issues will include their impact upon employers as well as employees. In addition. unresolved or potential issues for future consideration will be highlighted.

Personnel Actions

The law prohibits discrimination against women in hiring, promotion, discharge, or suspension on the basis of pregnancy or childbirth. The impact of this provision is that employers may not refuse to hire or promote a woman, who is otherwise fully qualified for a job, just because she happens to be or could become pregnant. Thus, questions pertaining to a woman's childbearing status would be considered illegal and invalid during the selection process.

Some employers have taken issue with the hiring provision of the law due to the hazardous nature of their business operation. Where physical conditions including chemical exposure, radiation, heat stress, vibration, and noise may endanger the reproductive capacity of a female worker, employers have elected to consciously screen out women of childbearing age as possible employees. On February 1, 1980, the EEOC and the United States Department of Labor issued Interpretive Guidelines on Employment Discrimination and Reproductive Hazards asserting that "an employer's policy of protecting female employees from reproductive hazards by depriving them of employment opportunities without any scientific data is a per-se violation of Title VII."[25] Thus, it appears that in the absence of sound research data that validates actual danger, employers may not discriminate against women on the basis of potential hazards.

Discharge and suspension based upon pregnancy are prohibited. The employer does have the right to transfer a woman to a less strenuous and/or hazardous assignment during her pregnancy, however. Further, the employer need not guarantee the woman's normal rate of pay. Her pay may be adjusted to a fair rate for the job duties required of the temporary assignment.

Leave and Reinstatement Policies

The Pregnancy Disability Amendment specifically prohibits employers from treating pregnancy, childbirth and related medical conditions in a manner different from their treatment of other disabilities. Thus, the Amendment requires that women, who have been disabled due to pregnancy, childbirth, or related medical conditions, be provided the same benefits as those provided other disabled workers. Among the benefits to which the employee would be entitled would be temporary and long term disability insurance, sick leave, and other forms of employee disability benefits.

In all respects, pregnant employees must be treated equally with other employees. However, the Amendment never requires the employer to give pregnant employees special treatment. If an employer provides no disability benefits or sick leave to other employees, he/she is not required to provide them to pregnant employees.

The Amendment disallows arbitrarily established policies regarding the commencement of maternity leave, prefering instead to have the issue decided on the basis of each individual's ability to work. Determination of ability to work has normally been left to the woman's physician, who would be in the best position to evaluate the medical consequences of continued employment. Employers have sometimes found, however, that the employee's physician's determination is even more liberal than their own previous leave policy. In such cases, when the employer is faced with an extended pay-out of sick leave and disability benefits, a second medical opinion, from a company-appointed medical expert, is being required prior to the granting of maternity leave.

Policies with regard to length of maternity leave are also affected by the new law. In the past, a majority of employers with "liberal" disability benefits provided for a duration of only six weeks for pregnancy, as compared with 26 weeks for sicknesses and injuries.[26] Other employers allowed a maximum of 15 to 26 weeks for such leave.[27] The length of maternity leave is now an issue to be determined by the woman's and/or the company's physician. Although the length of the leave may vary in individual cases, the woman will, for the most part, be paid only for the time a doctor certifies that she is disabled.[28]

Reinstatement procedures under the law require job availability, retention of pay rate, preservation of seniority ranking and other entitlements similar to those under any leave conditions. Under the terms of the Act, an employer is required to hold the employee's job open on the same basis as jobs held for employees on sick or diability leave. Once the employee returns to work from the pregnancy disability, the employer's policy of accruing and crediting seniority must be applied in the same manner for her as it would be for any other person who had been absent due to disability. Likewise, vacation accrual and pay increases will be applied in a manner similar to that for any other disability. It should be noted, however, than once a woman extends her leave beyond the time when she is disabled medically, the law no longer protects her job or her salary and her rights upon return to work are left to the discretion of her employer.[29]

Medical and Disability Benefit Payments

Under the Act, employers are bound to extend medical and disability benefits for childbirth to the same extent that coverage is provided for other medical conditions. Employers were given an initial "grace period" of 180 days after enactment of the Pregnancy Disability Amendment in which to comply (by April 29, 1979). Hence equalization of benefits for pregnancy related disability within existing plans was to occur within six months after October 31, 1978. Many employers initially expressed concern for what they felt would be a large increase in the cost of providing equality in benefits. These concerns proved to be unfounded as the Health Insurance Association of American estimated that the extension of health insurance coverage to pregnancy-related conditions of women employees and employee spouses would increase premiums by an average of 13 percent.[30] The comparatively low cost of pregnancy disability benefits was also underscored at Senate hearings regarding the proposed Amendment in April, 1977, by the Xerox Corporation, which has a liberal benefits program for its 42,000 employees (which include 11,000 women). In 1976, Xerox's total annual cost of pregnancy disability leaves was $746,542 or $17.77 per employee per year.[31] Other testimony at those hearings estimated that the cost of the benefit, when distributed over the nation's female working population, would equal $10 per female employee per year.[32]

Employees often share in the cost of their medical and disability benefits by payment to group health insurance plans. Increases in premiums resulting from the inclusion of pregnancy benefits have led some employees to complain about this cost when they can see no direct benefit to them in their own life situation. Employees whose spouses are past childbearing age, for example, charge that they are being discriminated against by having to pay higher medical insurance premiums. These charges have been answered with the assurance that employees under less costly group coverage subsidize many illnesses and conditions which may never affect them personally.

Pension Benefits

Just as it was once customary practice for employers to discriminate against pregnant women in the distribution of employment benefits so, too, did custom allow differentiation of pension benefits for females. For those women who stayed in the employing organization, overall benefits were sometimes lower for them than for their male counterparts. For example, retirement plans typically either required women to pay more into the system while working or required them to contribute the same sums as men to their pensions while they were working and then paid out lower monthly benefits to women in their retirement years. These practices were based upon the insurance industry's actuarial assumption that women, as a group, live about seven years longer than men and would thus need more money over a longer time period upon retirement.

The Manhart Case

Two significant Supreme Court cases have greatly influenced practice in the pension benefit area. The "pay-in" issue was addressed in 1978 in the Manhart case.[33] The employer-imposed requirement that women make greater contributions to its pension plan than men in similar positions was found to be an unlawful employment practice.[34] Title VII was applied to the case with the contention that the law "precludes treatment of individuals as simply components of a racial, religious, sexual or national class."[35] Instead, employees were to be treated as individuals without regard to sex in determining contribution provisions of pension systems.

The Norris Case

The "payout" issue was addressed in 1983 in the Norris case. [36] In that situation, female and male employees made equal contributions to pension funds that were administered by third party insurance companies. One of the pension plan's three pay-out options provided larger sums for men than women based upon the assumption that women, as a group, live longer than men. The Supreme Court reasoned that although this case varied from Manhart in that the plan was voluntary, operated by third party insurance companies, non-contributory for the employer, provided other non-discriminatory options and required equal contributions of male and female participants, it was still a violation of Title VII.[37] The Court found the Arizona retirement annuity option to be equivalent to the Manhart plan since a female employee desiring "monthly annuity retirement benefits equal to those of a similarly situated male employee. . .would have to make greater monthly contributions to the plan while working, just as in Manhart.[38] Thus, the Norris case extends Title VII coverage to situations in which an employer is involved in securing annuity benefits for employees. Unisex actuarial tables will be required and existing plans will need to be modified prospectively according to the Supreme Court's ruling.[39] This means that those benefits that are attributable to contributions made after the Court's decision will need to be calculated without regard to the sex of the employee.[40]

The Manhart and Norris cases illustrate the expanding nature of Title VII coverage. The fringe benefit area is subject to scrutiny for equality in coverage and impact upon employees. Clearly pension benefits in the private sector and at state and local levels will need to be developed and monitored with a concern for equity.

This chapter has provided a framework for understanding the social and legal background of the Pregnancy Disability Amendment of 1978. The major provisions of the law have been discussed along with their impact on employment policies. Related issues have been cited in order to fully inform human resource managers regarding the implications of the Act. A second benefit area, pension plan funding and disbursement has also been examined. Recent Supreme Court decisions indicate that this fringe benefit area provides a significant area for E.E.O. interpretation.

[1]   As of March. 1979, some 22 states and the District of Columbia required private employers to pay pregnancy benefits to women disabled by pregnancy according to S. Cavanaugh, "Pregnancy as a Discrimination Issue," Washington, DC, Library of Congress Issue Brief IB77039, Congressional Research Service, March 23, 1979, p. 2.

[2]   208 U.S. 412 (1908).

[3]   Ibid. at 421

[4]   Diane N. Westcott, "Employment and Unemployment in the First Half of 1981," Monthly Labor Review, August, 1981, p. 7.

[5]   U.S. Department of Labor Bureau of Labor Statistics, Handbook of Labor Statistics, Bulletin 2070, December, 1980, Table 59, p. 117.

[6]   U.S. Department of Labor Bureau of Labor Statistics, Perspectives on Working Women: A Datebook, Bulletin 2080, 1980, Table 35, p. 35.

[7]   Ibid. Table 44, p. 44.

[8]   Statement by Wendy Williams before the Subcommittee on Employment Opportunities (House) Committee on Education and Labor pt. 1, 95 Cong. 1st session p. 8 (1977).

[9]   C. L. Meacham, "Sex Discrimination in Employment--The Law: Where It Is and Where It's Going," in W.C. Hamner and F.L. Schmidt (eds.), Contemporary Problems in Personnel, (Chicago: St. Clair Press, 1977), p. 134-141. This reading was excerpted from Bringing Women Into Management by Gordon and Strober, McGraw- Hill, Inc., 1975.

[10]   Ibid.

[11]   400 U.S. 542 (1971).

[12]   400 U.S. at 544 (1970).

[13]   444 F.2d 1192 (7th Cir. 1971).

[14]   429 U.S. 125 (1976).

[15] 29 C.F.R. 1604 issued April 4, 1972.

[16] 429 U.S. 125 at 135.

[17] Ibid.

[18] 98 S. Ct. 347, 351 (1977).

[19] 434 U.S. at 141.

[20] PL 95-555 Sec. 1, 92 Stat.2076.42U.S.C. sec. 200(e) (k).

[21] United States Code Congressional and Administrative News, 95 Congress 2nd Session, Vol. 5 Legislative History (1978), p. 4749 at 4752-4753.

[22] PL 95-555 Sec. 1, 92 Stat.2076,42U.S.C. sec. 200(e) (k).

[23] United States Code Congressional and Administrative News 95 Congress 2nd Session, Vol. 5 Legislative History (1978), p. 4749 at 4752-4753.

[24] Newport News Shipbuilding and Dry Dock Co. v. E.E.O.C. 103 S.Ct. 2622 (1983).

[25] Hugh M. Fineran, "Title VII and Restrictions on Employment of Fertile Women," Labor Law Journal, April, 1980, p. 224.

[26] Paul S. Greenlaw and Diana L. Foderaro, "Some Practical Implications of the Pregnancy Discrimination Act," Personnel Journal, October, 1979, p. 681.

[27] "The Law About Pregnancy Leave," Working Woman, September, 1980, p. 50.

[28] Mary Schnack, "How Long A Maternity Leave Can Your Career Afford?", Working Woman, September, 1980, p. 50.

[29] Ibid.

[30] Lynne Olson, "Pregnancy Law Upsets Employers," The Sunday Sun, Baltimore, Maryland, April 22, 1979, p. A1.

[31] Senate Hearings, "Discrimination on the Basis of Pregnancy," Subcommittee on Labor of the Senate Committee on Human Resources, S. 995, April 26, 27, 29, 1977, p. 532, 536.

[32] Sally Palmer, "Pregnancy Benefits Pending," Working Woman, December, 1977, p. 88.

[33] City of Los Angeles Department of Water and Power v. Manhart, S.C. 137 (1978).

[34] Robert E. Nagle, "Eliminating Sex-Based Pension Features After Norris: The Alternatives Available to Plan Sponsors," Journal of Pension Planning and Compliance, October, 1983, p. 341.

[35] 435 U.S. at 708.

[36] Norris v. Arizona Governing Committee for Tax Deferred Annuity and Deferred Compensation Plans, 103 S.Ct. 3492 (1983).

[37] David W. Calton, "Sex Discrimination-Pensions-The Court Takes a Stand Arizona v. Norris," Wayne Law Review, 30:1329, 1984, p. 1336.

[38] Ibid. p. 1348.

[39] Ibid. p. 350-51.

[40] Nagle op. cit. p. 343.

Chapter IV

Review Questions

Equal Employment Opportunity and Employment Benefits

1. Why did the Supreme Court hold that the failure of employers to include pregnancy disability as a covered benefit did not constitute illegal sex discrimination?

2. Why did employers often exclude pregnancy as a disability under their health insurance plans?

3. What rules did Congress establish for the treatment of disabilities arising from pregnancy?

4. In 1978 Congress amended Title VII by adding the Pregnancy Disability Amendment hhich required employers to include pregnancy as a disability for female employees. An employer, to comply with the law, included pregnancy as a disability in its health insurance plan for female employees. The employer's insurance plan also covered the pregnancy of the spouses of male employees though the pregnancy coverage was less extensive than that provided for female employees. What legal issues could be raised against the employer's plan?

5. Under a deferred compensation pension plan developed by the state of Arizona, both male and female employees paid in the same contributions, but upon retirement the female employees received smaller payments because actuarial tables showed that women as a class have longer life expectancies than men. Was the plan administered in a discriminatory fashion because retired female employees received lower monthly payments than males who paid in the same amount of money?

Sexual   Harassment: A   Recently
Recognized Form of Employment Discrimination*

The issue of sexual harassment represents two
major challenges to employers in business and
government today. The first challenge is to understand
the legal background pertaining to this complex issue
including case law developments and interpretation of
E.E.O.C. guidelines. The second challenge for
employers is to put this legal framework into practice
via pro-active human resource management programs which
include policy formulation, information dissemination
and guidelines for action. This chapter will examine
and address these challenges.

Incidence

The incidence of sexual harassment in the
workplace today is sufficient to evoke employer
concern. A 1980 federal government survey of 23,000
workers with a response rate of 85 percent revealed
that 42 percent of female employees and 15 percent of
male employees had experienced some form of sexual
harassment over a two-year period.[1]

A sample survey of 700 Harvard Business Review
subscribers with a 25 percent return reported that 10
percent of respondents had witnessed serious forms of
sexual harassment leading to consequences such as loss
of a job or negative impact on a performance
evaluation.[2] Biles noted that "in the absence of
comparably rigorous studies in the private sector,
personnel managers should presume that a roughly
similar situation exists in their own companies."[3]

---

*This chapter first appeared as a paper by the authors,
entitled "Sexual Harassment: Legal and Policy Issues
for Employers of the 80's," published in the National
Proceedings of the American Business Law Association,
San Antonio, Texas, 1984, Jan W. Henkel, Editor.

Legal Background

Sexual harassment as a practice within the workplace is not a new phenomenon. Recognition of the practice as a legal problem is, however, relatively recent. The Federal Courts have found harassment to be a form of illegal Title VII sex discrimination (see Williams v. Saxbe,[4] Barnes v. Costle,[5] Bundy v. Jackson [6]. The Civil Rights Act of 1964 did not specifically encompass sexual harassment until the 1980 E.E.O.C. Guidelines discussed below. Thus, as a legal concern for employers, this issue is a recent one that is likely to develop through case law and interpretation throughout the 1980s.

Application of Title VII - The Loss of Tangible Benefits Standard

The landmark case on the application of Title VII remedies to sexual harassment is Williams v. Saxbe[7] decided at the end of 1976. Factually, the case is similar to three earlier cases which held that sexual harassment was not a form of sex discrimination under Title VII.[8] In this case the plaintiff alleged that because she rebuffed her supervisor's sexual advances he, in retaliation, reprimanded her, refused to consider her recommendations and ultimately fired her from her job with the Justice Department.

Judge Richley of the United States District Court for the District of Columbia found that the supervisor's sexual harassment of the plaintiff consituted a form of sex discrimination protectable under Title VII. Judge Richley reasoned that the plaintiff was subject to the harassment solely because of her sex. The defendant employer had argued that the plaintiff had not been the victim of sex discrimination as defined by Title VII because her supervisor's conduct reflected a personal attachment to her that was not gender based because male as well as female employees could be subject to the same type of harassment. In rejecting the defendant's arguments the judge concluded that unless the supervisor in question were a "bisexual" and engaged in similar conduct to both genders, gender based discrimination had taken place.[9]

In Barnes v. Costle[10] the D.C. Circuit Court was asked to decide if sexual harassment was a form of disparate treatment based on sex protectable under Title VII. The reasoning of the Court was very similar to that of the Saxbe case. The Court in finding that

the supervisor's sexual harassment was an illegal form
of sex discrimination under Title VII reasoned that

> a female employee "became the target of
> her superior's sexual desires because she
> was a woman, and was asked to bow to his
> demands as a price for holding her job
> (while) no male employee was susceptible
> to such an approach by a superior."[11]

The 1980 E.E.O.C. Guidelines on Sex Discrimination

The E.E.O.C. in response to the precedent that
had been established by the courts that sexual
harassment is a form of sex discrimination encompassed
by Title VII, formulated a set of guidelines defining
what types of conduct constitute illegal sexual
harassment. Specifically the guidelines state:

> Unwelcome sexual advances, requests
> for sexual favors, and other forms of
> physical conduct constitute sexual
> harassment when: (1) submission to such
> conduct is made either explicitly or
> implicitly a term or condition of an
> individual's employment, (2) submission to
> or rejection of such conduct by an
> individual is used as the basis for
> employment decisions affecting such
> individuals, (3) such conduct has the
> purpose or effect of unreasonably
> interfering with an individual's work
> performance or creating an intimidating,
> hostile, or offensive working
> environment.[12]

Court Interpretations - Atmosphere of Discrimination Theory

The decision in Bundy v. Jackson,[13] the first
case to come before the courts respecting the
application of the E.E.O.C.'s sexual harassment
guidelines represented a significant expansion of the
scope of the protection of Title VII as applied to
sexual harassment. A new legal issue was raised in the
Bundy case that had not been previously presented to
the courts. Bundy, unlike the plaintiffs in the
earlier cases, had not been denied any tangible job
benefits because of her refusal to bow to her
supervisor's sexual advances. Bundy's employer argued
that she was not entitled to relief under Title VII or

the E.E.O.C. guidelines because she had not been denied
any tangible job benefits. The Court rejected this
argument reasoning that "a condition of employment as
defined by Title VII can include the psychological and
emotional work environment . . . the sexually
stereotyped insults and demeaning propositions to which
she was undisputably subjected caused her anxiety and
debilitation."[14]

Though Bundy had not lost any tangible employment
benefits the Court reasoned that her employer's conduct
created an atmosphere of discrimination which can be
encompassed under category three of the E.E.O.C.
guidelines which state that sexual harassment can take
place if such harassment creates an intimidating,
hostile or offensive working environment.[15]

A category three violation was also found in
Brown v. City of Guthrie.[16] The plaintiff in this
case had suffered a type of sexual harassment similar
to Bundy's. In its holding the Court stated that
"sexual harassment that penetrates the workplace
(created) an intimidating, hostile or offensive working
environment should be deemed an impermissible condition
of employment."[17]

Employer Responsibility

Four provisions regarding the liability and
responsibilities of employers are contained in the
E.E.O.C. Guidelines: (1) an employer can be held
strictly liable for sexual harassment by its agents and
supervisory employees, (2) an employer can be held
liable for the harassment of employees by their co-
workers, (3) an employer can be held liable for the
harassment of employees by non-employees, and (4) the
employer can be held liable if it has actual or
constructive notice of the problem and fails to take
appropriate corrective measures.[18]

Supervisory Personnel

The circumstances under which an employer can be
held liable for the acts of its agents was formulated
in the case of Tomkins v. Public Service and Gas
Company. In that case the Court held that:

Title VII is violated when a supervisor,
with the actual or constructive knowledge
of his employer, makes sexual advances or
demands toward a subordinate employee and

conditions that employee's job on a
favorable response to those advances or
demands and the employer does not take
prompt or appropriate remedial action
after acquiring such knowledge.[19]

Co-Workers

While it is clear that a person in a supervisory
position who can condition employment on the granting
of sexual favors is acting on behalf of the employer,
it may seem less clear if a co-worker who engages in
sexual harassment is engaging in conduct in violation
of Title VII. However, Subsection (d) of the E.E.O.C.
Guidelines does make provision for co-worker harassment
in the following terms:

> With respect to conduct between fellow
> employees, an employer is responsible for
> acts of sexual harassment in the workplace
> where the employer, its agents or
> supervisory employees, know or should have
> known of the conduct, unless it can be
> shown that it took immediate and
> appropriate corrective action.[20]

Summarizing the present state of the law on this
subject Lynn McLain has observed that:

> Both prior judicial and E.E.O.C. decisions
> unanimously agree that the employer is
> responsible for harassment by a mere co-
> worker only if the employer has been made
> actually or constructively aware of the
> problem and has failed to take prompt,
> appropriate action. Arguably, the
> inaction of the employer, his or
> her failure to take reasonable remedial
> steps. acts as ratification of the
> harassment.[21]

Non-Employees

The E.E.O.C. Guidelines also provide for employer
liability for sexual harassment by non-employees. Non-
employees can include independent contractors, sales
and repair persons, customers, clients or patients as
well as non-invitees such as trespassers. Such
liability can be imposed if the employer tolerated or
condoned the conduct. Employers can be held liable for

the acts of non-employees if the following conditions are met under the E.E.O.C. Guidelines:

> An employer may also be responsible for acts of non-employees, with respect to sexual harassment of employees in the workplace, where the employer, its agents or supervisory personnel know or should have known of the conduct and fail to take immediate corrective action.[22]

The first case upholding the guidelines' imposition of liability for non-employee sexual harassment was E.E.O.C. v. Sage Realty Corporation.[23] The plaintiff in that case was required to wear a poncho-like uniform which was so skimpy that portions of the plaintiff's thighs and buttocks were exposed. The sexually provocative costume resulted in the plaintiff being subjected to lewd comments and gestures by passersby in the lobby. She complained to her employer about the dress requirement but was told that she would either have to wear what they told her to wear or lose her job. She refused to wear the costume and was discharged.

The employer raised the defense that employers have a right to impose dress requirements on employees. The Court refused to accept this argument holding that the right of employers to impose dress standards did not give them the unfettered right to force employees to wear sexually revealing clothing.

Employer Defenses to Liability

In order for an allegation of sexual harassment to be successful the employee must allege that: (1) submission to sexual advances by a supervisor was a term or condition of employment, (2) rejection of sexual advances affected the victim's employment, and (3) employees of the opposite sex were not affected in the same way.[24]

In order for an employer to defend against liability for employee sexual harassment, the employer must intervene when he/she knows that a supervisor has made or is making sexual demands on a subordinate employee as a term or condition of employment. The intervention must be prompt and appropriate. Merely establishing a policy prohibiting retaliation for rejection of sexual advances could not protect an employer from liability for a supervisor's conduct.[25]

The major case to address this issue is Miller v. Bank of America.[26] Miller, the plaintiff, had complained of sexual harassment on the ground that her supervisor promised her a better job if she was sexually cooperative. In its defense the Bank of America asserted that it should not be held liable because it had an established policy prohibiting sexual harassment and an in-house grievance mechanism. The bank also claimed that the plaintiff had not processed her allegations through the channels provided for by the company. The bank's defense prevailed in a district court proceeding.

On appeal the bank was ultimately held liable on a strict liability theory. The Court of Appeals reversed the District Court's findings by the use of an analogy from the law of torts. The Court reasoned that a taxi company would be held liable for a pedestrian's injuries caused by the negligence of one of its drivers even though the taxi company had developed a safe driving training program and provided for the dismissal of drivers who drove negligently. Using a strict liability standard the Court held the Bank of America liable despite the existence of company regulations specifically prohibiting sexual harassment.[27]

E.E.O.C. Guidelines Regarding Sexual Orientation

In order for an act of sexual harassment to come under the umbrella of Title VII and the E.E.O.C. Guidelines the act must be committed by an individual who is either heterosexual or homosexual. If the harasser is a bisexual, the harassment would not constitute an actual Title VII violation. Thus, under the E.E.O.C. sexual orientation guidelines sexual harassment by a bisexual individual of either sex would not constitute a violation of Title VII because the victim was not the object of the illegal conduct on the basis of sex.[28]

Professors Paul S. Greenlaw and John P. Kohl[29] have developed a sexual harassment matrix. They include in the matrix, blackmail as a form of sexual harassment that could, in the future, be a type of sexual harassment recognized by the E.E.O.C.'s Guidelines. They point out that under present E.E.O.C. Guidelines verbal harassment can constitute an illegal form of sexual harassment. The inclusion of such actionable behavior may open the door for the blackmailing of supervisors for favors such as raises, promotions and so on when the employee may tell the supervisor's superior that he/she was verbally harassed. In light of the potential for abuse of the law Greenlaw and Kohl argue that the E.E.O.C. will have to develop specific guidelines for dealing with such situations.

Implementation of the Law by Employers

Policy Formulation

Sample policy statements are available in the literature. See for example Biles, 1981[30] and Petersen, 1982.[31] An example of a general statement was presented by Faucher and McCulloch:

> Our courts have decided that racial, ethnic, religious, or sexual harassment on the job is against the law. This company prohibits verbal and physical harassment of its employees based on race, national origin, religion or sex.[32]

Although this policy statement is generally inclusive, it fails to outline specifically proscribed behaviors. Many organizations have found that more detailed policies help to clarify employer and supervisor role expectations.

The employer should determine the extent to which a detailed statement is needed for his/her organization and then develop a written policy that includes the following:
   a. a strong statement indicating employer disapproval of sexual harassment.
   b. a definition of the term sexual harassment
   c. a list of verbal and non-verbal behaviors considered undesirable conduct
   d. an outlined procedure whereby an employee may seek relief from sexual harassment
   e. support for individual employee rights and protection from reprisal under this policy

Dissemination

The employer's sexual harassment policy statement must have the full endorsement and support of top management. The policy should be circulated and discussed at management meetings from the top of the organization on down. In its discussion, it should be made clear that sexual harassment policy implementation will henceforth be considered as part of the normal performance review for all managers.

This step should be accompanied by action from the Human Resource Management function. Personnel officers should prepare and distribute interpretive guidelines for action (if needed), hold informal discussions of the policy with employee groups, and generally see that all employees have been exposed to the policy by a specific time deadline. The policy should be incorporated into all new employee orientation sessions. One personnel officer should be the designated coordinator for this policy so that employees know who to seek out for advice and counsel.

Implementation

A written grievance procedure should be clearly stated to deal with sexual harassment cases. Since such cases often occur between supervisor and subordinate, the usual first step in a negotiated grievance procedure may not be appropriate. The first step should, more realistically, involve an informal exploration of the situation wherein the employee meets with the personnel officer responsible for sexual harassment policy.[33]

This initial session should be verbal, guarantee anonymity (if possible) and provide the supportive couseling necessary to draw out the facts. Focus should be upon the who, what, where and why of the incident or case history, identification of any witnesses or other similarly affected employees, and a discussion of work or personality issues that could be related to the situation under review. The employee should not be promised any one specific response at this point. Rather, the next steps in the investigatory procedure should be outlined and the employee should be asked to call immediately if other confrontations occur.

Linenberger lists the ten factors that the E.E.O.C. looks at in determining what constitutes sexual harassment. These factors should also be considered by the personnel officer before deciding upon a course of action. They are: severity of conduct (physical versus verbal behavior), number and frequency of encounters, apparent intent of the perpetrator, relationship of the parties, provocation of the victim, apparent effect on the victim, response of the victim, working environment, public or private nature of the encounter and male/female ratios in the workplace.[34]

After discussing the situation with the employee, the personnel officer should then examine the employee's and the supervisor's personnel records. Sculnick suggests that the following areas of inquiry should be considered: prior disciplinary warnings, denial of merit increases because of supervisory ratings, refusal of promotion or transfer by the supervisor, other allegations of improper conduct against this supervisor, discipline administration in a discriminatory manner, application of corporate personnel policy in a uniformly fair and consistent manner.[35]

After consideration of the facts thus obtained, the personnel officer should interview the supervisor to hear his/her side of the story. Sculnick provides a comprehensive guide to this interview.[36] The aim of this session is simply to collect more factual data and to gain an understanding of any differences in perception between the employees involved in the sexual harassment case.

At this point, the judgment of the personnel officer is crucial. The offense must be reviewed in terms of severity (behavior, intent and frequency) and certainty of its occurrence. Each incident must be judged on its own merits and a fair determination made. In the most severe cases supported by strong evidence, "possible action steps include dismissal, demotion, transfer of the accused, and/or restoration of complainant's work record where unjustly blemished."[37] More moderate cases might be handled via written warning or disciplinary notice while mild cases might merit no record and no action beyond a sexual harassment policy review session with the supervisor involved. Schulnick notes that the most difficult decisions may have to be made with inconclusive cases. He notes that "at a minimum, the company should warn the supervisor that it considers the allegations extremely serious, and although the facts are controverted, such conduct is forbidden and will not be tolerated."[38] Documentation of the incident should be maintained for a set time frame, such as one year, in case a similar situation occurs. In all circumstances, steps should be taken to protect the complainant from reprisals.

Prevention

Perhaps the best way to avoid sexual harassment problems is to sensitize all employees to the employer's strong stand on the sexual harassment issue through word and deed. Training sessions for supervisors can help. Sample case histories can be openly discussed and concerns about interactions with subordinates can be ventilated in a candid, supportive training environment. Such discussions can often help to identify areas in need of clarification for all supervisors. Keeping in mind that co-workers can be quilty of sexual harassment as well, it is important to get reminders out to all workers from time to time. House organs and bulletin boards can be used to convey company policy on sexual harassments as appropriate.

[1] U.S. Merit Systems Protection Review Board, "Sexual Harassment in the Federal Workplace: Is It a Problem"? Washington, DC, U.S. Government Printing Office, 1981.

[2] Eliza G. C. Collins and Timothy B. Blodgett, "Sexual Harassment . . . Some See It Some Won't," Harvard Business Review, (March-April 1981), pp. 77-95.

[3] George E. Biles, "A Program Guide for Preventing Sexual Harassment in the Workplace," Personnel Administrator, (June 1981), pp. 49-56.

[4] 413 F. Suppl. 654 (D.D.C. 1976).

[5] 561 F.2d 983 (C.A.D.C. 1977).

[6] 641 F.2d 934 (D.C. Cir. 1981).

[7] 413 F. Supp. 654 (D.D.C. 1976).

[8] See Baines v. Train-13 F.E.P. Cases (123 D.D.C. 1974), Corne v. Bausch and Lomb, Inc.- 300 F. Supp. 161, Tomkins v. Public Service Electric and Gas Company-422 F. Supp. 553 (D.N.J. 1976), rev'd 568 F.2d 1044 (1977).

[9] 413 F. Supp. 655 (D.D.C. 1976).

[10] Op. Cit., Note 5.

[11] 561 F.2d 990.

[12] 29 C.F.R. Part 1604, 11, 1980.

[13] Op. Cit., Note 6.

[14] Ibid.

[15] Ibid. at 961. See also: George E. Stevens, "The Cruel Trilemma, Sexual Harassment Under Title VII and the Tangible Job Benefits," American Business Law Journal, Vol. 20, 1982, pp. 109-117.

[16] 22 F.E.P. Cases 1627 (1980).

[17] Ibid. 1628.

[18] 29 C.F.R. Sec. 1604.11(d) (e) (f).

[19] 568 F.2d 1044 (3rd Cir. 1977).

[20] 45 Fed. Reg. 74, 677 (1980), 29 C.F.R. Sec. 1604.11(d).

[21] Lynn McClain, "The E.E.O.C. Sexual Harassment Guidelines Welcome Advances Under Title VII," University of Baltimore Law Review. Vol. 10, 1981, pp. 323-324.

[22] 45 Fed. Reg. 74.677 (1980), 29 C.F.R. Sec. 1604.11(e).

[23] 507 F. Supp. 599, (S.D.N.Y., 1981).

[24] 42 U.S.C. Sec. 2000(e)-2(a) (1)-(2).

[25] "Sexual Harassment," CCH - Commerce Clearing House Inc. Human Resource Management - Equal Employment Opportunity, Sec. 2141.

[26] 418 F. Supp. 233 (N.D. California 1976).

[27] 600 F.2d 211 (CA-9, 1979).

[28] Paul S. Greenlaw and John P. Kohl, "Harassment: Homosexuality, Bisexuality and Blackmail," Personnel Administrator, June 1981, p. 60.

[29] Ibid. p. 61.

[30] George E. Biles, "A Program Guide for Preventing Sexual Harassment in the Workplace," Personnel Administrator, (June 1981), pp. 49-56.

[31] Donald J. Petersen and Douglas Massengill, "Sexual Harassment - A Growing Problem in the Workplace," Personnel Administrator, (October 1982), pp. 79-89.

[32] M. D. Faucher and K. McCulloch, "Sexual Harassment in the Workplace: What Should the Employer Do"? E.E.O. Today, 1978 Vol. 5, p. 38.

[33] Petersen, op. cit., pp. 79-89.

[34] Patricia Linenberger and Timothy J. Keaveny, "Sexual Harassment in Employment," Human Resource Management, (Spring 1981), pp. 11-17.

[35] Michael V. Sculnick, "A Policy and Procedure for Handling Harassment Complaints," <u>Employment Relations Forum</u>, (Summer 1983), pp. 161-175.

[36] <u>Ibid.</u>

[37] Gary N. Powell, "Sexual Harassment, Confronting the Issue of Definition, <u>Business Horizons</u>, (July-August 1983), pp. 24-28.

[38] Sculnick, <u>op</u>. <u>cit</u>. pp. 161-175.

Chapter V

Review Questions

Sexual Harassment

1. What elements must be established to prove the existence of sexual harassment?

2. Does an employee have to be fired to maintain a cause of action under Title VII claiming sexual harassment?

3. Distinguish between the loss of tangible benefits standard and the atmosphere of discrimination theory.

4. Explain an employer's liability for acts of sexual discrimination in the following circumstances:
   (a) acts of its agents or supervisory personnel
   (b) acts of co-workers
   (c) acts of non-employees

5. What measures should an employer take to avoid sexual harassment charges?

Chapter VI

Executive Orders and Affirmative Action

Executive Orders

Title VII of the Civil Rights Act as amended in 1972 pertains to private sector employers as well as to state and local governments. In order to bring virtually the entire nation's labor force under the umbrella of employment discrimination policy, President Johnson issued Executive Order 11246 in 1965. As originally issued, the Order prohibited discrimination on the basis of race, color, creed or national origin. It was amended via E.O. 11375 in 1967 to prohibit discrimination on the basis of sex. These Orders apply to the Federal government and Federal contractors and subcontractors.

E.O. 11246 required government contractors with 50 or more employees and a contract of $50,000 or more to develop and implement affirmative action plans (AAP's). The four major steps in developing AAP's include:

1. analysis of the employment of minority and female employees
2. identification of deficiences
3. establishment of employment goals
4. development of methods for meeting the goals

At first, the contractor receiving an award had up to 120 days to submit a plan. Later, plans were sometimes required in order to bid on a contract. Under the Reagan Administration, AAP requirements have been relaxed in some situations to the extent that paperwork and reporting requirements have been reduced and employers are asked to have affirmative action plans and to be able to produce documentation if requested.

Enforcement

Under the terms of the Executive Order, the Secretary of Labor is charged with supervising and coordinating the activities of the federal contracting agencies. The Secretary of Labor has established the Office of Federal Contract Compliance Programs (O.F.C.C.P.) to administer the order. The O.F.C.C.P. requires and reviews employers' affirmative action plans. Numerical goals and timetables for the recruitment and promotion of women and minorities are expected as part of AAP's. These goals and timetables can be adjusted for the availability of qualified applicants in the employer's Standard Metropolitan Statistical Area (SMSA) or relevant labor market. Failure to follow O.F.C.C.P. guidelines can result in cancellation or termination of a contract or prosecution in court.

The Office of Federal Contract Compliance Programs, in addition to supervising government contracts in general, also has set up special programs for federal construction contractors. Essentially there are two types of programs. The so-called "hometown" plans are voluntary area-wide affirmative action agreements entered into by local representatives of minority groups, construction unions and contractors. Among the cities where "hometown" plans have been in effect are Chicago, Pittsburgh, and Boston.

If a "hometown" plan cannot be voluntarily agreed to, then a Philadelphia Plan will be mandated. Under the Philadelphia Plan, bidders on federal construction contracts which exceed $500,000 are required to present specific hiring goals which are determined on the basis of the population distribution of the area. The presentation of these specific goals is a precondition to the receipt of a contract.

The legality of the so-called Philadelphia Plan was brought into question in the Contractors Association of Eastern Pennsylvania vs. Schultz[1] on the ground that the Plan's requirement of "quota" or preferential hiring was in conflict with the prohibition of such preferential hiring as set forth in Title VII. In holding the Plan constitutional, the Circuit Court of Appeals asserted:

> To read 703(a) (that section of Title VII which prohibits preferential hiring) in the manner suggested by the plaintiffs we would have to attribute to Congress the intention of freezing the status quo and to foreclose remedial action under the authority designed to overcome existing evils.[2]

Though the Philadelphia Plan was upheld by the courts, the Labor Department eliminated mandatory affirmative action plans for Philadelphia, Washington, DC, San Francisco, Atlanta, and Camden, NJ. A substitute for the Philadelphia Plan will be an

O.F.C.C.P. requirement that affirmative action specifications will be incorporated into basic construction contracts. The forty-two voluntarily agreed to "hometown plans" which were in effect in 1977 were not altered by the Labor Department's decision.

Affirmative Action by Executive Order

In 1973 the O.F.C.P. issued a set of guidelines for non-construction contractors and government agencies for judging and developing affirmative action programs. The guidelines for employers were set out in Order No. 4 which stated that:

> An acceptable affirmative action program must include an analysis of areas within which the contractor is deficient in the utilization of minority groups and women, and further goals and timetables to which the contractor's good faith effort must be directed to correct the deficiencies and, thus to increase materially the utilization of minorities and women, at all levels and in all segments of his work force where deficiencies exist.[3]

Furthermore an affirmative action program must include the following:

(1) An analysis of all major job categories at a facility must be conducted with explanations if minority group members are being underutilized in job categories.

(2) Goals, timetables and affirmative action commitments must be designed to correct any identifiable deficiencies. When deficiencies exist the regulations require the contractor to create specific goals and timetables as part of his written affirmative action program.

(3) Support data for the programs and an analysis shall be maintained as part of the contractor's affirmative action program; and

(4) Contractors shall direct special attention to six work categories identified by the government as most likely to show underutilization of minorities - officials and managers, professionals, technicians, sales workers, office and clerical workers and skilled craftsmen.[4]

The guidelines under Order No. 4 also provide suggested procedures for use in establishing, implementing and judging an acceptable affirmative action program. The contracts must consider such factors as:

(1) The minority population of the labor area surrounding the facility and the size of the minority work force.

(2) The general availability of minorities having requisite skills in the immediate labor area and in an area in which the contractor can reasonably recruit.

(3) The availability of promotable minority employees within the contractor's organization.

(4) The anticipated expansion, contraction and turnover in the labor force.

(5) The existance of training institutions capable of training minorities in the requisite skills.

(6) The degree of training which the contractor is reasonably able to undertake as a means of making all job classes available to minorities.[5]

The Executive Orders discussed above differ in several respects from Title VII. Unlike Title VII the Executive Orders require that contractors take "affirmative action" to ensure equal employment opportunity. While Title VII has an explicit prohibition against preferential or "quota hiring" no such prohibition is to be found in the various Executive Orders. Additionally, unlike Title VII, the Executive Orders do not provide an exemption for employment policies instituted pursuant to a bona fide seniority system.

Affirmative Action by Court Order

Affirmative action may be required by Executive Order or by Court order as a remedy in a Title VII discrimination case or it may be undertaken voluntarily by an employer. "Affirmative action" quidelines present complex dilemmas for management decision makers who often are faced with the prospect of being sued whether they comply or not with federal guidelines. If they fail to fully comply with federal affirmative action guidelines, they may be subject to suit by minority workers. If concerted action is taken by management to recruit minority members, suits may be brought by whites claiming reverse discrimination. As one scholar has observed:

> Whether the Constitution is color blind or permits "benign" racial classifications is controversial because of the wide-spread and generally accurate public perception that the issue affects daily life in fundamental matters: it has a direct impact on the practical matter of who gets ahead in America in the competition for jobs, admission to professional schools and other areas of personal advancement.[6]

This question was squarely presented in Kaiser Aluminum Co. v. Weber.[7] In 1974 the union and the company had signed a collective bargaining agreement which provided that half the positions in their new craft training program would be reserved for blacks. Weber, who was white and more senior than the black employees who were accepted into the program, claimed "reverse discrimination."

The agreement between Kaiser Aluminum Company and the steel-workers' union was held to be within the spirit of Title VII because under the law:

(1) Employers and unions are not required to institute such programs, but those who wish to voluntarily create such programs are not prohibited from doing so by statute.

(2) The plan was limited in scope and duration in that when the imbalance was rectified the reverse discrimination would discontinue.

(3) Since the company was without a history of prior discrimination, it may voluntarily adopt such a program to correct a racial imbalance caused not by the company's actions, but by the general practice of racial discrimination.[8]

Recent Developments Under the Reagan Administration

In August of 1985, officials of the Reagan Administration circulated a draft of a proposed amendment to Lyndon Johnson's executive order and the subsequent efforts of the Labor Department to enforce the order through the requirement that federal contractors meet specific goals and time tables with

97

respect to the hiring and promotion of minorities and women.

The Reagan Administration proposal states that:

"The Secretary of Labor shall immediately revoke all regulations and guidelines promulgated pursuant to Executive Order 11246 if they require companies doing business with the government to use numerical quotas, goals, ratios or objectives."

The proposed amendment also states that:

"Nothing in this executive order shall be interpreted to require or provide a legal basis for a government contractor or subcontractor to utilize any numerical quota, goal or ratio, or otherwise discriminate against or grant any preference to any individual or group on the basis of race, color, religion, sex or national origin with respect to any aspect of employment."

Anne B. Fisher writing for Fortune magazine assesses the potential impact of this Executive Order in the following terms: "In effect (the proposed Executive Order) would make numerical goals and time tables voluntary . . . which would weaken the legal basis for such programs, possibly exposing employers to a blizzard of suits by white male employees or job applicants claiming that affirmative action has discriminated against them."[9]

The Reagan Administration Justice Department is seeking to justify a curtailment of its responsibility to enforce "affirmative action" through a broad reading of a 1984 decision of the Supreme Court.

In Firefighters Local 1784 v. Stotts[10] the Supreme Court ruled that the city of Memphis, Tennessee had acted illegally by laying off white workers with more seniority than less senior black workers for the purpose of maintaining a set racial quota of black employees. The city argued that they had acted pursuant to the requirements of the law because the layoff of the more senior white workers was necessary to achieve an adequate racial balance in the work force. The Supreme Court held that the city's conduct was discriminatory because the white workers had acquired their seniority through a bona-fide seniority system. Basing its decision in this case on earlier cases the court held that the preservation of a racial balance in the workplace under an affirmative action plan is subordinate to the preservation of a bona-fide seniority system.

Since the Supreme Court did not specifically address the issue of the legality of quotas to hiring, but only focused on the issue as applied to layoffs, the Reagan Administration Justice Department has taken the position that the decision makes illegal any preference on the basis of sex or race in the hiring as well as the layoff of workers. While the scope of the Stotts decision has not been addressed by the Supreme Court, six Courts of Appeal have refused to follow the Justice Department's broad interpretation of the Stotts decision.[11]

On the Supreme Court's calendar for the 1985-86 term is a case in which the Supreme Court may decide to address the current issues pertaining to the legal status of affirmative action.[12]

Support for the Reagan Administration's plan is not widespread in the business community according to a survey conducted by a consulting firm called Brigington Resources Counselors. A recent survey conducted by the group showed that 95% of the 140 companies surveyed would still use hiring goals even if such goals were no longer required by government.[13]

Implications for Employers

Relaxation of record keeping and reporting requirements does not negate the obligation of employers to implement the spirit of affirmative action in Human Resource Management activities, regardless of whether the direct scrutiny of the O.F.C.C.P. or the E.E.O.C. is involved. Many states now require Affirmative Action Plans of their contractors: thus the concept is still a viable one. Employers must balance the demands of AAP's with business necessity and find a posture that works for their particular organization.

Realistic recruitment goals should be established based upon the availability of qualified applicants. Employers should expand recruitment efforts insofar as practical to reach the widest possible applicant pool. Recruiter visits to minority schools and ads in minority publications may aid in these efforts.

Selection methods should be validated for all applicants as well as minority groups. Differential cut-off scores on employment tests may be considered if reasons for reduced performance can reasonably be attributed to factors other than capability (perhaps a language or cultural difference, for example). Interviewers should be trained to avoid questions that might imply a bias on the part of the employer with regard to race, color, religion, sex or national origin.

Placement of minorities and women should be throughout the organization. Care should be given to avoiding job ghettos to which minorities and women are assigned with little chance for upward mobility. Training opportunities and career paths should work toward the advancement of qualified members of previously disadvantaged groups.

Affirmative Action in Special Cases

The Handicapped

Recognizing that handicapped persons are a minority subject to discrimination Congress enacted The Vocational Rehabilitation Act of 1973. This law prohibits discrimination in employment against handicapped persons by employers who receive federal contracts or assistance. Section 504 of the Act states:

> No otherwise qualified handicapped individual . . . shall, solely by reason of his handicap, be excluded from the participation in, be denied the benefits of, or be subject to discrimination under any program or activity receiving Federal financial assistance.

Under the law, handicap not only refers to physical impairments but also to mental problems (retardation and emotional disorders) and illnesses such as diabetes, heart disease, epilepsy and cancer.[14] Individuals with a history of alcoholism and drug dependency are also considered "handicapped" under the Act; however, a 1978 amendment "provides that an employer does not have to give an employment opportunity to job applicants with a history of alcohol or drug abuse where it can be shown that the prior addiction or abuse would prevent successful performance on the job applied for."[15]

The law is similar to Executive Order 11246 in that it applies only to government contractors, it requires affirmative action, and it is enforced by the O.F.C.C.P. within the Department of Labor. Unlike Executive Orders, however, it does not require goals and timetables.[16] Under the Act Congress required all private employers with federal contracts over $2,500 to take affirmative action to recruit, hire and advance qualified handicapped persons. Companies with one hundred or more employees and holding a federal contract for more than $100,000 must maintain their affirmative action plans for the handicapped. In addition to the above, employers must make a reasonable accommodation for their handicapped workers.

Reasonable accomodations include required, expected and recommended actions by employers.[17] Required accomodations include eliminating qualifications such as passing a physical exam if not job related and unprejudiced treatment of handicapped persons in the hiring decision. Recipients of federal funds are expected to provide reasonable job access such as wheelchair ramps, braille signs in elevators, etc. and job design that insofar as possible removes tasks that a handicapped person cannot perform. Recommended actions include employee assistance programs such as counseling for alcoholism, drug dependency or psychological problems.

In sum, reasonable accomodation does not mean that the employee must sacrifice productivity by tolerating lower job performance from handicapped employees, nor does it mean that the employer must endanger others by placing a handicapped employee in a position where the handicap would pose a threat. Indeed, being free of certain handicaps may be a 'bona fide occupational qualification'.[18]

Vietnam Veterans

The Vietnam Era Veterans Readjustment Act of 1974 prohibited discrimination against disabled veterans and Vietnam era veterans. It requires affirmative action programs of Federal contractors. Executive Order 11701 (1973) applied to the federal government on the same issue. Enforcement is through the Office of Federal Contract Compliance Programs.

[1] 442 F.2d 159.

[2] Ibid. at 173.

[3] U.S. Equal Employment Opportunity
Commission, Affirmative Action and Equal Employment
Opportunity: A Guidebook for Employers, Vol. 2,
Washington, DC, Government Printing Office (1974), p.
D-28.

[4] U.S. Equal Employment Opportunity
Commission, Affirmative Action and Equal Employment: A
Guidebook for Employers, Vol. 1, Washington, DC,
Government Printing Office, 1974, pp. 16-17.

[5] Howard J.Anderson,Primer of Equal Employment
Opportunity, The Bureau of National Affairs, Inc.,
Washington, D.C. (1978), p. 86.

[6] Steven Wisotsky, "Reverse Discrimination,"
The Florida Bar Journal, Vol. 54, No. 3, March, 1980,
p. 197.

[7] 443 U.S. 193 (1979).

[8] Ibid., pp. 194-195.

[9] Anne B. Fisher, Business Likely to Hire by
the Numbers, Fortune, Vol. 112, No. 6, September 16,
1985, p. 27.

[10] 104 S. Ct. 2576 (1984).

[11] Fisher Op. Cit., p. 30.

[12] "The Court: Back to the Future," Newsweek,
October 14, 1985.

[13] Fisher, Op. Cit., p. 28.

[14] Leslie BB. Milk, "The Key to Job
Accomodations," Personnel Administrator, 24:1, 1979,
p. 31-33, 38.

[15] Henry R. Cheeseman, The Legal and Regulatory
Environment of Business, Macmillan Publishing Company,
New York, NY (1985), p. 767.

[16] Public Law 93-112, 87 Stat. 335. U.S. Code Congressional and Administrative News.

[17] James Ledvinka, Federal Regulation of Personnel and Human Resource Management, Kent Publishing Company, Boston, MA (1982), p. 79-80.

[18] Ibid.. p. 81.

Chapter VI

Review Questions

Executive Orders and Affirmative Action

1. How do the provisions of the Executive Orders differ from Title VII?

2. What types of data must an affirmative action program contain?

3. What does the term reasonable accommodation mean under the Rehabilitation Act of 1973?

4. A federal agency rejected an applicant suffering from dyslexia (a reading disability) on the basis of a written test alone. What legal issues could the rejected applicant raise?

Chapter VII

Emerging Issues in Discrimination Law

This chapter highlights two additional areas of importance to employment discrimination. Although the law is 18 years old, the Age Discrimination in Employment Act has recently become more of a concern to employers due to increasing claims, it is therefore worth reviewing. The traditional employer's right to termination-at-will. is challenged by every one of the laws discussed in this book. This fact has resulted in recommendations for changes in policy and behavior in this second area of focus. The discrimination arena is truly dynamic and complex. These recent developments must be understood and effectively managed.

The Age Discrimination in Employment Act

Age is not a protected category under Title VII of the Civil Rights Act of 1964. In 1967, The Age Discrimination in Employment Act (ADEA) was enacted by Congress to address age as a specific category of discrimination. When enacted, the Act covered persons between the ages of 40 and 65. In 1978, Congress amended the Act to include nonfederal employees up to age 70. There is an exclusion from the Act of executives with pension entitlements of $27,000 or more per year.

The Act covers persons or organizations who have twenty or more employees whose business affects interstate commerce. It covers employment agencies with regard to all their clients even if the employer for whom the agency is finding an employee is not covered by ADEA.[1] According to Section 4 of the Act, those covered under the law are forbidden to:

(1) Fail or refuse to hire, discharge, or in any other way discriminate against any individual because of his age with respect to compensation, terms, conditions or privileges of employment.

(2) To limit, segregate, or classify an employee in any way that would deprive him of job opportunities or adversely affect his employment status because of age.

(3) Reduce the wage rate of the employee to comply with the Act.

(4) Advertisements must not indicate any preference, limitation, specification based on age in any notices or advertisements for employment.

The Act does permit employers to refuse to hire persons above a certain age, if age can be demonstrated to be a "bona fide" occupational qualification for the successful performance of the duties required. B.F.O.Q.'s based on age have been upheld for air traffic controllers, pilots and agents of the F.B.I.[1] Persons under 40 or over 70 do not receive age discrimination protection under the Act.

The Age Discrimination in Employment Act can be differentiated from Title VII in three ways:

(1) Only one group is protected (people age 40-70) and others are not, therefore reverse discrimination is not prohibited.

(2) Retirement is regulated in that forced retirement before age 70 is illegal.

(3) The Act does allow employers to differentiate among candidates or employees on some "reasonable factor other than age."[2]

Reasonable factors might include job requirements for speed, strength, safety, visual acuity and reaction time any of which might screen out a larger proportion of people between the ages of 40 and 70. The E.E.O.C. regulations interpreting the Act "say that job relatedness is required of practices having an adverse impact on people in the protected age group."[3]

Claims of age discrimination have been labeled the "third wave of employment opportunity cases" promising to add unique aspects to EEO issues not found in race and sex discrimination cases.[4] In recent years, the number of cases filed has quadrupled over the number filed six years ago. Much of this activity is atributed to an attitude change among white middle class males who are now more prone to seek redress and to the ADEA Amendments of 1978.[5] The three major changes resulting from the Amendments include first that "claimants in age discrimination cases (unlike those involved in race or sex bias cases) may request jury trials"[6] which are more likely to result in sympathetic awards. Second, "procedural roadblocks were amended out of the act"[7] thus substantially reducing the burden of the litigation process for the claimant. Third, the amendments negated earlier case law on ADEA leaving more questions open to challenge. On July 1, 1979, "the power to enforce the amended ADEA was shifted from the Department of Labor to the E.E.O.C."[8] Since that time, guidelines have been issued that allow the EEOC "more latitude to interpret the law on a case by case basis."[9]

Two authors have provided helpful guidelines to employers for dealing with the Law.[10] Some of these guidelines are summarized as follows:

(1) Personnel decisions should be based upon appropriate guidelines, validation studies and current professional standards with "systematically documented analyses of true worker competence."

(2) Sensitize managers to the potential consequences of any reference to age.

(3) Human resource departments should frequently and widely disseminate information on EEO and antidiscriminatory policies.

(4) Keep current on ADEA. The authors particularly recommend a column by the General Counsel for the National Commission on Aging which appears in the journal Aging and Work.

(5) When an employee between 40 and 70 is not offered a job or is replaced, be ready and able to show that the replacement was more qualified.

(6) If an employee is offered a transfer or demotion in place of firing or layoff, document this in writing.

(7) If early retirement is offered and accepted, consider having the employee sign a waiver of rights to sue under ADEA.

(8) Keep up-to-date records on the age of workers to identify affirmative action concerns and be sensitive to potential ADEA trouble spots as personnel actions occur.

Employment at Will

Since the 19th century, business history in the United States has demonstrated the employer's right to discharge employees at any time and for any reason "as long as no statute or agreement existed to limit such action."[11] Thus, employees have served at the will of the employer offering loyalty and obedience in return for a livelihood. Either party could end the employer-employee relationship at any time, thus the phrase termination-at-will has often been used to describe this relationship. However, it is generally agreed that termination generally has far more traumatic consequences upon an individual's career than resignation.

The laws discussed in the preceding chapters clearly represent challenges to the termination-at-will doctrine. Beginning in 1935 with the Wagner Act, labor laws were the first to restrict management's discretion in the discharge of employees sympathetic to labor activities and issues. By far the most dramatic changes have come with Title VII of the Civil Rights Act of 1964, the Equal Employment Opportunity Amendments of 1972, the Age Discrimination in Employment Act of 1967, and the Vocational Rehabilitation Act of 1973. Employers can no longer terminate at will without first considering whether the employee is a member of a protected class and whether appropriate, non-discriminatory actions have been taken.

Court rulings have generally found in favor of employees who were promised either orally or in writing that termination would only occur for "just cause."

"If companies still believe that the employment at will doctrine shields them from legal liability, it appears that they are on shakey ground. According to developing law, a claim to set aside a discharge may rest on one or more of three grounds:

(1) the discharge violates a clear public policy of the state, enunciated by the state constitution, statutes, regulations or decisional law;
(2) the discharge breaches a covenant of good faith and fair dealing implied by the court in the employment relationship; or

(3) the discharge violates an implied or
stated condition of employment,
namely to fire only for 'just
cause'."[12]

Current case law and legislation appear to support the
concept that "once employed, a worker has a right to a
job unless he fails to live up to his part of the
bargain . . . or the employer has . . . a business
slow-down"[13] thus providing just cause for
termination. The right to a job is implied from the
employment contract whether stated or implied.

Employers must be aware of the developing legal
environment of employment at will. Each new law or
regulation that impacts upon employment discrimination
clearly restricts an employer's discretion in hiring
and firing decisions. This means that employers must
review all employment documents, handbooks, and
orientation programs to be sure that the statements
made about performance and continued employment are
those that the employer can live with in light of all
the other restrictions on decisions in the employment
at will area.

Chapter VII Footnotes

[1] Henry R. Cheeseman, The Legal and Regulatory Environment of Business, MacMillan Publishing Company, New York: NY (1985), p. 761.

[2] James Ledvinka, Federal Regulation of Personnel and Human Resource Management, Kent Publishing Company, Boston, Massachusetts (1982), p. 75-76.

[3] Ibid., p. 76.

[4] R.S. Greenberger, "Fired Employees in 40s Filing More Bias Suits," Wall Street Journal, (October 9, 1981), p. 31.

[5] Robert A. Snyder and Billie Brandon, "Riding the Third Wave: Staying on Top of ADEA Complaints," Personnel Administrator, (February 1983), p. 41.

[6] Ibid.

[7] Ibid., p. 42.

[8] Ibid.

[9] Ibid., p. 43.

[10] Ibid., p. 43-47.

[11] Maria Leonard, "Challenges to the Termination-at-Will Doctrine," Personnel Administrator, (February 1983), p. 49.

[12] Ibid., p. 52.

[13] Ibid., p. 55.

Chapter VII

Review Questions

Emerging Issues in Discrimination Law

1. In what ways can the Age Discrimination Act be differentiated from Title VII?

2. What is the employment-at-will doctrine?

3. What implications does the employment-at-will doctrine have for employer free speech?

Index

About the Authors

Dr. Richard Trotter is an Associate Professor of Management at the University of Baltimore. He holds a Ph.D. from the University of Pennsylvania and a J.D. from Rutgers University. He is a member of the Pennsylvania Bar and is admitted to practice before the United States Supreme Court. Dr. Trotter is also a labor arbitrator who is listed on the panel of the American Arbitration Association. His publications include articles on various aspects of employment discrimination law. At present he is completing a book on the regulatory environment of business to be published by Houghton-Mifflin and Company.

Dr. Susan Rawson Zacur is currently Associate Professor of Management at the University of Baltimore. She received a B.A. from Simmons College and an M.B.A. and a D.B.A. from the University of Maryland. Her books and articles focus on Human Resource Management issues. Dr. Zacur has done training for clients such as I.B.M., Westinghouse, T. Rowe Price Associates, and The National Aquarium.